It Happened on the Underground Railroad

It Happened In Series

It Happened on the Underground Railroad

Remarkable Events That Shaped History

Second Edition

Tricia Martineau Wagner

Globe
Pequot

GUILFORD, CONNECTICUT

Globe Pequot

An imprint of Rowman & Littlefield

Distributed by NATIONAL BOOK NETWORK

Front cover photo: Orelia Alexia Franks, ex-slave, Beaumont. Library of Congress

Text design by Nancy Freeborn
Map by M. A. Dubé © Morris Book Publishing, LLC

British Library Cataloguing in Publication Information Available

Library of Congress Cataloging-in-Publication Data

Wagner, Tricia Martineau.
It happened on the Underground Railroad : remarkable events that shaped history / Tricia Martineau Wagner.—Second edition.
pages cm
Includes bibliographical references and index.
ISBN 978-1-4930-1574-0 (paperback : alkaline paper) — ISBN 978-1-4930-1587-0 (electronic)
1. Underground Railroad—Anecdotes. 2. Fugitive slaves—United States—Anecdotes. 3. Abolitionists—United States—Anecdotes. I. Title.
E450.W14 2015
973.7'115—dc23   2015008463

∞™ The paper used in this publication meets the minimum requirements of American National Standard for Information Sciences—Permanence of Paper for Printed Library Materials, ANSI/NISO Z39.48-1992.

For Lois Gallaher Holmes,
truly a blessing in our family

I consider involuntary slavery a never-failing fountain of the grossest immorality, and one of the deepest sources of human misery; it hangs like the mantle of night over our republic, and shrouds its rising glories.

—*Reverend John Rankin, 1826*

CONTENTS

CONTENTS

ACKNOWLEDGMENTS

I gratefully acknowledge the assistance of the following people, without whom I could not have written this book:

- Diane Miller, National Program Manager, National Underground Network to Freedom, National Park Service, Omaha, Nebraska, for providing updated statistics on the Underground Railroad.

- Michelle Lanier, director of the North Carolina African American Heritage Commission, Raleigh, for her research assistance with Mary Walker and the connections she provided.

- Those who pointed me in the right direction when beginning the research for this second edition, including Dr. Tom Hanchett, staff historian at the Levine Museum of the New South, Charlotte, North Carolina; Caroline Manning, registrar at the Harvey B. Gantt Center for African-American Arts & Culture, Charlotte; Leslie Kesler, library aide at the Robinson-Spangler Carolina Room, Charlotte Mecklenburg Library, Charlotte; and Stephanie Hardy, site manager at the Historic Stagville State Historic Site, Durham, North Carolina.

- Caroline R. Miller of the Bracken County Historical Society, Brooksville, Kentucky, for her invaluable research on Arnold Gragston, Reverend John Rankin, and John P. Parker, and also for compiling census records from the Freedom Center in Covington, Kentucky.

ACKNOWLEDGMENTS

- Anne-Marie Rachman, Michigan State University Library, Special Collections, for her research expertise, especially the information she uncovered about James Lindsey Smith.

- Marla Baxter, Assistant Director of Tourism & Renaissance on Main; Lynn David of the Museum Center; and Betty Coutant of the *Mason County Beat* in Maysville, Kentucky, all of whom shared their information on Arnold Gragston.

- Betty Campbell, president of the Board of Trustees for Ripley Heritage, Inc., and member of the Board of Trustees for the John P. Parker Historical Society, Inc., for sharing research on Reverend John Rankin. Her presentation on John P. Parker inspired me to write about him.

- Major Ronald J. Rice of the Maysville Police Department, for sharing research material on Arnold Gragston and for inviting me to visit the Broadway Christian Church in Dover, Kentucky.

- Doris E. Onorato at the Van Allen House Heritage Center in Mount Pleasant, Iowa, for collecting a plethora of information on Ruel Daggs.

- Mary Savage, the museum board historian for the Lewelling House and Quaker Museum, and Faye Heartsill, president of the board at the Lewelling Quaker Museum, Iowa, for sharing material on Ruel Daggs.

- John Zeller, research historian for the Antislavery and Underground Railroad Project of the State Historical Society of Iowa, for general information on the workings of the Underground Railroad in Iowa.

- Joan Beaubian, president of the New Bedford Historical Society and cofounder of the Massachusetts Underground Railroad Network, for providing information on Nathan and Polly Johnson.

ACKNOWLEDGMENTS

- Jennifer Bergeron of the Barney Ford House Museum in Breckenridge, Colorado, for research on Barney Ford.

- Courtney Oppel, my editor at Globe Pequot Press, as well as Erin H. Turner and Allen Jones, who assisted with editing for the first edition of this book.

- The staffs at the Hege Library at Guilford College in Greensboro, North Carolina; the University Library at the University of North Carolina–Chapel Hill; and the Rare Book Manuscripts and Special Collections Library, Duke University, Durham, North Carolina, for their research assistance.

- Gaye E. Gindy, Sylvania historian, Sylvania, Ohio, for her willingness to share her wealth of information on the Lathrop and Harroun families. Her research did much to prevent the Lathrop House from being razed.

- Polly Cooper, Sylvania Area Historical Society, Sylvania, Ohio, and Catherine Martineau, Esq., for information on the Lathrop House.

- Sharon Sacksteder, FSIL, for sharing the story of Miss Edith May Haviland, her remarkable fifth-grade teacher at Lincoln Elementary School in Adrian, Michigan. The work of Miss Haviland's abolitionist ancestor, Laura Smith Haviland, was thus brought to my attention.

- Beth R. Olsen, author and long-distance friend, who suggested that I write this book, for her encouragement and her research assistance on William and Ellen Craft, and for helping to unravel the quilt myth and its connection to the Underground Railroad. I also thank her daughters, Andrea Cramer and Julia Smoot, for the same.

ACKNOWLEDGMENTS

- Melissa Johnson, for her friendship and continuous support and for accompanying me on visits to Underground Railroad sites.

- Lorie Helms, Beth Wilson, Anita Sanchez Fitzgerald, Nancy Mills, Kathryn Zychowicz Rahal, Pam Walker, and Joan Rush for their interest and friendship, as well as Beth White, my sister and friend.

- My husband, Mark, for his technical support and unending patience, and our children, Kelsey and Mitch. Thank you for being such a loving family.

INTRODUCTION

Far from being truly underground, or even a railroad, the Underground Railroad was in fact a loosely organized network of individuals who assisted slaves as they escaped bondage in pre–Civil War America. Between the 1820s and 1860s, an untold number of enslaved African Americans fled over multiple land and water routes to freedom. Slaves from the border states stretching along the Ohio River had an increased chance of success due to their closeness to free soil in the North. Many continued on to Canada. Slaves from Texas crossed the Rio Grande into Mexico. Slaves from Georgia, South Carolina, and Alabama escaped to live with the Seminole Indians in Florida or the Caribbean. Some groups of fugitives set up self-sufficient "maroon societies," living out their lives in remote areas such as the Great Dismal Swamp along the Virginia–North Carolina border.

As rail transportation became increasingly popular in the 1830s, metaphors emerged to describe the clandestine movement of slaves on the run. "Passengers" escaped along "lines," transported by "conductors" and aided by "agents" who had made the arrangements. The "stations" were safe houses where the fugitives hid and were offered food, clothing, and temporary shelter.

There are several claims as to the origin of the term "Underground Railroad." One involves a slave named Tice Davids, who ran away from Kentucky to Ripley, Ohio, in 1831. When Davids's owner could find no trace of him, he said that his slave had "gone off on an underground road." By the 1840s the Underground Railroad evolved into a secret network of individuals, families, and small groups taking in slaves who came to them from the previous station and making sure they made it to the next.

It was never a large-scale operation with membership or national regulation. Most "conductors" knew only a handful of people involved with the railroad, and very few were familiar with an entire route. Any form of participation was recognized as an act of civil disobedience. Given the constant threat of fines, imprisonment, or even death, it was work that had to be done in the utmost secrecy. While accurate statistics are unavailable (to protect the participants, most of the paperwork was either nonexistent or destroyed), it is estimated that less than 2 percent of America's four million enslaved people escaped to freedom. The "father of the Underground Railroad," William Still, in the course of his work for the Pennsylvania Anti-slavery Society, did manage to preserve an accurate record. Much of what we know today about the Railroad is due to his diligence.

The period of greatest activity for the Underground Railroad began with the passage of the Fugitive Slave Law of 1850. With this new law, slave owners could legally pursue their runaways into the free states of the Union, capturing them on free soil and forcibly taking them back to a slave state. Ironically, the passage of this law only strengthened the abolitionist movement and bolstered the determination of those activists involved in the Underground Railroad.

Even aided by individuals associated with the Underground Railroad, slaves on the run often had to rely on their own resources. Most conductors could take them only as far as the next station (anywhere from one to thirty miles). To outwit the bounty hunters and their bloodhounds, they sometimes camouflaged their scent by running through a river or a creek, or a snake-infested swamp. Sometimes they doubled back to throw off the hunt. Often runaways were not dressed appropriately and suffered from hunger and other privations. Very few had money, and most were unable to read.

Typically traveling at night, fugitives might get a head start if they left on a Sunday or a holiday, when their absence might not immediately be noticed. Young men statistically had the highest chance of success. Unencumbered by family, they could cover greater distances. They were also more often familiar with the surrounding area, especially if they had been hired out on various jobs around the community. Once they connected with a "conductor," however, they typically put their lives in the hands of a complete stranger. Uncertain of whom they could trust, fugitive slaves were in constant fear of being caught. If they were captured, punishment was swift, and they were often whipped or sold. Being sent to the Deep South, with its reputation for cruel treatment, was a threat slaves feared as much as whipping.

If their light skin allowed them to "pass" for white, escapees might look for a nice set of clothes and try to board a train or boat to freedom. An ingenious fugitive even had himself mailed north. Some fugitives who successfully escaped sought out black communities where they could blend in with those already free. However, the illegal slave trade was a highly profitable business, which gave way to the kidnapping of free blacks. Men, women, and children—either born free or escaped from bondage—carried their free papers with them, yet still were not always safe. The border states with large black populations were particularly vulnerable to kidnapping because of their proximity to slave states.

Harriet Tubman, Frederick Douglass, Levi Coffin, and Sojourner Truth are a few of the famous names associated with the Underground Railroad, but there are a host of unsung heroes as well, all with inspirational stories. Individuals such as John P. Parker, Seth Concklin, Peter Still, and the Rankin family often risked their own freedom and health by assisting others in their escapes from bondage. Slaves like Solomon Northup, Harriet Jacobs, and Mary

Walker had to wait years until the opportunity and assistance to escape presented itself.

Historically there has been an overemphasis on the participation of white abolitionists in the Underground Railroad movement, and an underrepresentation of involvement by African Americans. The true stories contained in *It Happened on the Underground Railroad* attempt to shed light on black agency.

The institution of slavery, from its start in 1619 to the end of the Civil War in 1865, is an unspeakable stain on America's history. This book is a tribute to the courage of those—enslaved and free, black and white, women and men, young and old—who devoted their lives to helping others obtain their freedom.

This map can only suggest the general direction that runaways took from slave states to free territory. There were almost as many routes as there were freedom-seekers. Areas near the borders between North and South, such as the Ohio River and the Chesapeake Bay, saw greater numbers and much more Underground Railroad activity than did the routes from Florida to the Caribbean or from Texas to Mexico.

SELECTED ROUTES ON THE
UNDERGROUND RAILROAD

BAKER'S SPECIAL
Nathan and Polly Johnson,
New Bedford Caterers

1834

The residents of New Bedford, Massachusetts, were already lining up to taste Mary "Polly" Johnson's iced cakes and ice cream delicacies. The thirty-five-year-old widow, who had remarried a man nine years her junior, had been to culinary school in Paris, France, and had just opened a confectionary shop in town. Nathan Johnson, Polly's husband, ran his successful catering business serving the city's elite. The townspeople who frequented the cake, confectionary, and catering shop at 23 Seventh Street would have been shocked had they known what was really going on behind the scenes of the bakery.

Polly and Nathan Johnson were both free blacks who had worked for Quaker employers before becoming financially independent. In time they purchased a block of residential and commercial properties on Seventh Street. Their two-story Federal-style house was well known—for several reasons.

Polly Johnson was widely accepted in white society. She was described as a "fair mulatto, always lady-like and pleasant." Indeed, Polly charmed customers who entered her shop, who most likely mistook her smirk for a smile. Polly's candies, sponge and loaf cakes, cookies, and ice cream were highly sought after. Together the Johnsons catered wedding receptions for New Bedford's wealthiest families, threw cake-and-ice-cream parties, and hosted all sorts of celebrations.

Nathan and Polly Johnson enjoyed a fine reputation, but they were well-known among abolitionists for their clandestine operation as well. No slave-holding families suspected that the Johnsons were harboring fugitives and forwarding them on to the next station on the Underground Railroad. For over thirty years, none of the aristocratic members of New Bedford white society ever realized that the money they spent at the bakery was being used to aid fugitive slaves, nor that runaways were actually hiding inside the bakery itself.

Having a function catered by the Johnsons was a huge draw. In 1844 when Wendell Phillips, president of the American Anti-slavery Society, was asked to come speak in New Bedford, he was enticed by being told that "Polly Johnson will freeze her best ice and ice her best cakes." Countless fancy partygoers in New Bedford who hired the Johnsons unknowingly provided funds for the town's Underground Railroad network.

New Bedford, Massachusetts, was a small, bustling port city and an attractive location for blacks, both free and fugitive. Nathan had begun working for Charles Morgan, an investor in the whaling industry. Polly began as a domestic servant in Morgan's home. As free blacks, they were proud of the fact that their city had contained no slaves since 1785.

In the mid-1800s New Bedford's major industries, the maritime and whaling trades, provided job opportunities to blacks. Sea captains sympathetic to runaway slaves often transported them north from southern ports. These escapees usually found ready employment in town. The owners of the Seventh Street properties, Polly and Nathan Johnson, as agents on the Underground Railroad, often assisted New Bedford's fugitives—upwards of seven hundred between 1840 and 1860.

In 1834 Nathan and Polly took in five black boarders who had formerly belonged to a Georgia plantation owner. They began educating them, and upon their master's death three years later, the Johnsons took legal action to see that the former slaves were not remanded to slavery by claimants to the man's will.

In September 1838 a twenty-year-old man named Frederick Augustus Washington Bailey dressed as a sailor and escaped on a train with borrowed free papers. He then took the steamer *John W. Richmond* to New York. His fiancée, Anna Murray, a free black woman from Baltimore, arrived and they were married on September 15. Two days later Frederick and his new bride, Anna, arrived safely at the Johnsons' doorstep, courtesy of New York's Underground Railroad.

Nathan Johnson lent the penniless newlyweds $2 to retrieve their luggage, which was being held by the stage driver until they paid for their passage. The destitute couple were welcomed into the Johnsons' home, where they lived for one year. Frederick had taken the surname Johnson in New York, but Nathan advised he take a new name. "Johnson" had become a surname often taken by fugitives and might suggest they were not free blacks. Nathan suggested the name Douglas from a character in Sir Walter Scott's poem "The Lady of the Lake," which he was currently reading. This Frederick did, adding an *s*, and thus Frederick Douglass was born.

Douglass found employment refitting ships in New Bedford, and went on to become one of the most significant figures in American history. A famous orator, abolitionist leader, and advisor to President Abraham Lincoln, Frederick Douglass was perhaps the nineteenth century's most effective American voice for equal rights.

In the late 1840s the Johnsons suffered a reversal of fortunes, and Nathan moved to California in 1849, searching for gold. During his twenty-year absence, Polly successfully managed their heavily mortgaged properties and businesses.

Polly Johnson lived in the house at 21 Seventh Street until her death in 1871 at age eighty-seven. Nathan died in the home at the age of eighty-three. Their granddaughter, Mary J. Buchanan, lived in the house until 1891. Upon her death in 1918, she designated that the income from the Seventh Street Johnson properties be used for the general uplift of the black race in New Bedford. The monies from the sale of the properties were donated to the Massachusetts Institute of Technology for the purpose of educating "deserving and ambitious young men of color, of respectable northern parentage, in whatever department of physics they may elect, as being best adapted to their capabilities."

Today this same location houses the New Bedford Historical Society, an organization dedicated to preserving the rich history of African Americans.

SEVEN YEARS IN HIDING
Harriet Ann Jacobs's Confinement

1835

Harriet lay silently entombed in her dark, tiny hiding space, wondering how her life had taken such a turn for the worse. The small sloping garret above her grandmother's storeroom measured roughly nine feet long, seven feet wide, and just three feet high at the tallest point. Little did Harriet know when she crawled into that stuffy, cramped enclosure as a fugitive slave in the summer of 1835 that she would spend the next seven years there.

"I was born a slave; but I never knew till six years of happy childhood had passed away," recalled Harriet Ann Jacobs. She and her younger brother had lived in a modest home with both parents even though they were owned by different families. Her mother, Delilah, belonged to Margaret Horniblow. Her father, Elijah Jacobs, was the slave of Andrew Knox, whose plantation was several miles away. It was her father's earnings from his carpentry skills that allowed them the privilege of living together, but it was not to last.

Edenton was a colonial seaport on the shallow inlet waters of the Albemarle Sound in northeastern North Carolina. Harriet had lived there for all of her twenty-two years. Edenton lay 70 miles south of Norfolk, Virginia; 140 miles east of Raleigh, North Carolina; and 300 miles to freedom.

After her mother's death, six-year-old Harriet and her four-year-old brother, John, went to live with her mother's mistress, Margaret Horniblow. Just as Harriet was adjusting to her new life, her father died the following year. Over the next six years, Mistress Horniblow taught Harriet to read, write, and sew—seemingly she was a favored slave.

Harriet was convinced she would be given her freedom when Mistress Horniblow died. Instead, at the reading of the will, twelve-year-old Harriet dejectedly discovered she was just a piece of property like the rest of the slaves. Harriet had been willed to her mistress's three-year-old niece, Mary Matilda Norcom—along with Mistress Horniblow's bureau and work table. A stunned Harriet must have wondered what could possibly be worse than being given away and owned by a three-year-old. She soon found out—Dr. James Norcom, young Mary Matilda's father. It was he who had caused Harriet to be on the run.

Dr. Norcom took Harriet into his care until Mary Matilda came of age. Dr. and Mrs. Norcom were harsh masters to their twenty slaves, who were often ill-fed, ill-clothed, and mistreated. Fortunately, Harriet's dear grandmother, Molly Horniblow, lived nearby. She was a proud, free black woman who had long operated an after-hours bakery to save money to buy her family's freedom. Whenever Harriet and her brother John passed their grandmother's house, she snuck them baked sweets.

Harriet did her best to please Mrs. Norcom—and not displease Dr. Norcom—but as Harriet matured that became increasingly difficult. Dr. Norcom, in his fifties, was a respected physician in

Edenton. What was not so respectable were his intentions toward fifteen-year-old Harriet.

Dr. Norcom, a full forty years older than Harriet, had already fathered eleven slave children. Harriet was not about to let that happen to her. Yet, Dr. Norcom was relentless with his advances. Harriet refused to submit despite the favored treatment Dr. Norcom offered her. Nor did she bend under his threats of violence. Mrs. Norcom's jealousy, suspicion, and anger made Harriet's life miserable.

When Harriet was sixteen, Dr. Norcom refused to give her permission to marry a free black man. He was a carpenter in town who had offered to buy Harriet, but Dr. Norcom would not sell her at any price. In time Harriet found the sympathy of a family friend, a white lawyer named Samuel Tredwell Sawyer, who lived near her grandmother. Harriet responded to his affections, trusting he genuinely cared for her. Through him she devised a plan to thwart Dr. Norcom's unrelenting harassment.

Harriet's romantic involvement with Mr. Sawyer resulted in the birth of a child. Harriet figured Dr. Norcom would become so irate that he would sell her and then Mr. Sawyer could buy her freedom. Her plan failed. Harriet and her son, Joseph, lived with her grandmother, who disapproved of her granddaughter's actions. Dr. Norcom continued to pursue Harriet with letters and visits.

In 1833, when Harriet was eighteen, she had another child with Mr. Sawyer, a girl named Louisa Matilda. Harriet cried at the birth of her daughter, claiming, "Slavery is terrible for men, but it is far more terrible for women." In retaliation for having another child with Mr. Sawyer, Dr. Norcom sent Harriet six miles away to his son's cotton plantation to work as a house servant. To further punish Harriet, Dr. Norcom threatened to send her children to work as field slaves far from her and her free grandmother's protection.

So in June of 1835, Harriet ran away. She thought that if she were gone, Dr. Norcom would not be able to use her children against her and he would sell them. She planned to ask their father, Mr. Sawyer, to then buy their freedom.

Harriet endured several tension-filled months as she stayed with friends, both black and white, until a permanent hiding place could be secured. In the interim, Dr. Norcom put Harriet's two children, her brother John, and her aunt in jail in Edenton in an attempt to have them reveal where Harriet was hiding. They were eventually released without giving up any such knowledge. Meanwhile, Dr. Norcom posted a newspaper ad:

$100 REWARD

WILL be given for the apprehension and delivery of my Servant Girl HARRIET. She is a light mulatto, 21 years of age, about 5 feet 4 inches high, of a thick and corpulent habit, having on her head a thick covering of black hair that curls naturally, but which can be easily combed straight. She speaks easily and fluently, and has an agreeable carriage and address. Being a good seamstress, she has been accustomed to dress well, has a variety of very fine clothes, made in the prevailing fashion, and will probably appear, if abroad, tricked out in gay and fashionable finery. As this girl absconded from the plantation of my son without any known cause or provocation, it is probable she designs to transport herself to the North.

The above reward, with all reasonable charges, will be given for apprehending her, or securing her in any prison or jail within the U. States.

All persons are hereby forewarned against harboring
or entertaining her, or being in any way instrumental in
her escape, under the most rigorous penalties of the law.
JAMES NORCOM.
Edenton, N.C. June 30

An obsessed Dr. Norcom left for New York in search of Harriet. He sold Harriet's children and her brother, John, for $2,500. A slave trader bought them—on behalf of the children's father, Samuel Tredwell Sawyer. Sawyer gave the children to their grandmother. Feeling duped, Dr. Norcom's anger served only to intensify his search for Harriet.

A relative and family friend helped Harriet hide out, and she alternately spent two nights aboard a docked boat and two days in a mosquito- and snake-infested swamp. Harriet then donned a sailor's disguise, blackened her face with charcoal, and was led—of all places—back to her grandmother's house.

That's when Harriet was hurried into her hiding place: the sloping garret above her grandmother's garage. Harriet used a gimlet to bore holes in the wood to allow some air in and to provide a view to peek outside. Though stifling hot in the summer, wet in the spring, and freezing in the winter, it seemed more bearable than succumbing to Dr. Norcom's repeated advances.

Six-year-old Joseph and two-year-old Louisa Matilda had no idea their brokenhearted mother was watching over them from her hiding place. Harriet dared not to reveal herself to them, fearing Dr. Norcom was not above bribing her children for information on their mother's whereabouts.

When the coast was clear, Harriet was occasionally let out at night to exercise her legs. She passed the time reading the Bible and sewing clothes for her children. Harriet wrote letters to Dr. Norcom and her grandmother and had a friend postmark them from New York, to trick Dr. Norcom as to her whereabouts. Hidden away, Harriet watched her children from afar for seven long years, unable to hold them for fear of being discovered.

Mr. Sawyer was elected a North Carolina congressman and eventually moved to Washington, DC. He and his wife adopted Harriet's son, Joseph, and found a home for Louisa Matilda with a relative. Harriet's brother, John, became Mr. Sawyer's assistant, but when he saw his chance to run off, he did.

In 1842 Harriet ended her years of confinement and made a water escape. Her uncle and a family friend paid an exorbitant amount to secure passage with a trustworthy captain aboard a boat bound for Philadelphia. After disembarking, Harriet traveled by railway to New York, where she was soon reunited with her daughter and her brother John, who had previously moved north. A year later, her son, Joseph, joined the family in Boston.

For the next ten years, Harriet Ann Jacobs lived as a fugitive slave, but in a much wider arena. She moved between New York and Boston, working as a nursemaid for the family of Nathaniel Parker Willis, noted author, poet, and editor. Harriet was forced to keep on the move because the Norcom family continued to seek her out in an effort to re-enslave her.

Dr. Norcom's death in 1850 did not end Harriet's ordeal. His three-year-old daughter, Mary Matilda, whom Harriet had been willed to, had grown up. Bolstered by the Fugitive Slave Act of 1850, Mary Matilda and her husband attempted to recapture Harriet. They claimed Dr. Norcom had never been Harriet's legal owner and felt she was still their rightful property. Nor did they feel Dr. Norcom had any right to sell her children as his property either. (Dr. Norcom had also sold Harriet's brother, John, who had been "on loan" from his mother-in-law.)

In 1843 Harriet joined her brother, John S. Jacobs, in Rochester, New York. By 1849 Harriet and her brother worked in Rochester's Anti-slavery Office and Reading Room. Her antislavery work brought her in contact with abolitionists such as Frederick Douglass and Amy Post. Post encouraged Harriet to write about her experiences to strengthen the antislavery cause in the United States and England. Harriet agreed, thinking women especially could appreciate the difficult position into which slave women were forced by their masters.

In 1852 Nathaniel Parker Willis's second wife, Cornelia Grinnell Willis, bought Harriet's freedom, hoping to end the Norcoms' relentless pursuit of Harriet. Although Harriet was grateful, she had secretly always wanted to take her freedom, feeling no one had the right to buy or sell another human.

In 1861 Harriet Ann Jacobs self-published *Incidents in the Life of a Slave Girl*, using a pseudonym and changing names to protect those who helped her escape on land and sea. The start of the Civil War overshadowed the book's release, but the following year the book was published in England as *The Deeper Wrong*. The delicate nature of Jacobs's text in exposing the oppression slave women suffered at the hands of their male slave owners, coupled with the author's true identity not being made known, perhaps prevented the book from selling as well as Jacobs and the publisher had hoped.

Harriet continuously labored for the cause of oppressed black people. She offered relief work for freedmen in Washington, DC; Alexandria, Virginia; and Savannah, Georgia. She also started a school in Alexandria and operated a boardinghouse in Cambridge, Massachusetts. Harriet died in 1897, feeling she had done her best for eighty-four years to pursue freedom for herself and her children as well as expose the evils of slavery.

Harriet Ann Jacobs's book, the first fugitive slave narrative authored by a female in America, was lost in obscurity for over one hundred years. In 1973 *Incidents in the Life of a Slave Girl* was re-released in the United States when the women's and civil rights movements gained momentum.

THE DEVIL
Lindsey Payne's Longest Run

1838

Lindsey Payne's life savings of $3.50 jingled in his pocket as he took off on a limping run for the James Smith plantation. If he didn't make it in time, his two friends, Zip and Lorenzo, would leave without him. News that Zip had been purchased by a Georgia trader had necessitated an immediate escape. Eighteen-year-old Lindsey had little time to pack a bundle of clothes, some corn cakes, and bacon to sustain him on their journey on that May morning in 1838.

Lindsey's lame leg had kept him from laboring in the cotton fields, but now it was an enormous disadvantage. A childhood injury crippled him when a wood pile shifted and crushed his leg. Despite his mother's pleading, Mistress Sarah Langston had refused to seek proper medical attention. Now that he needed to cover the two-mile distance in record time, he was especially embittered. He would force his leg to carry him to the agreed-upon rendezvous point. Lindsey Payne had had enough of cruel masters and mistresses.

Lindsey reached Zip and Lorenzo just in time. He was glad to be leaving Heathsville, Virginia, where he was hired out as a shoemaker. But he was also leaving behind eleven siblings in Northumberland County. Realistically he held little hope of ever seeing them again, but that was the price of freedom.

The fugitives headed north in a boat they had confiscated along the Cone River and then continued on foot, covering some 250 miles. When it became apparent that the slower-paced Lindsey could not keep up with his two companions, they decided to split up. The two able-bodied men needed to strike out on their own to prevent all three from being captured.

A despondent Lindsey understood, but wept to himself at being left behind. Lurching on alone, Lindsey fought against despair until a terrifying experience changed his outlook.

At 3:00 a.m. on May 8, the ground shook under Lindsey and a strange thunder rumbled in the distance. He could see nothing in the dark. The horrific noise was coming around the bend. An iron monster reared its ugly head, spouting fire and smoke, screaming furiously on its quick approach. Lindsey had never seen a train before. He scrambled up a steep bank, thinking, "The Devil is about to burn me up. Farewell! Farewell!" With that, he passed out.

When he awoke, he was alone in the quiet dark. His imagination began to run away with him. He was sure that he heard the hoofbeats of "paddy-rollers" (patrollers, or night watchmen) coming after him. But no, it was only his own heart racing wildly. Lindsey resumed his journey.

Around noon he heard the Devil returning, caught on its set of metal tracks, wheels turning and steam pouring forth, choking and wailing. Behind it was a series of wagon-like roofed boxes the Devil carried with rows of white faces in the windows. "Wagons that he carries the souls to hell with," Lindsey thought. Still terrified, he was relieved to see that the Devil was not after black people, and grateful not to have been taken.

Continuing on, Lindsey eventually arrived at New Castle, Delaware, where he was somehow reunited with Lorenzo and Zip. The three fugitives planned to take a steamer up the Delaware River to Philadelphia, since traveling on foot was not expeditious. In New Castle, however, blacks came under scrutiny. The law forbade passage on steamboats without proof of free status—and securing free papers would be impossible. So the three runaways mustered the confident air of free black men. They looked straight ahead and walked up the steamship's gangplank clear to the ticket counter and purchased three tickets to Philadelphia. Miraculously, no one stopped to question them.

They arrived in Philadelphia on Thursday afternoon. Lindsey decided to stay in the United States, while Zip and Lorenzo boarded a ship to Europe to try their luck abroad.

In Philadelphia Lindsey was directed to a black shoemaker named Simpson to inquire about work. After a long conversation, Lindsey admitted he was a runaway. By luck, Simpson was an agent on the Underground Railroad. Simpson took him home, where he was welcomed by the shoemaker's family, fed well, and hidden overnight. The next day Simpson set Lindsey up with other contacts.

Friday morning, his sixth day on the run, Lindsey was put aboard a steamer to New York City with a letter of introduction to David Ruggles, a black printer and the secretary of the New York Vigilance Committee, part of an Anti-slavery Society organization that assisted fugitive slaves. Departing from New York three days later, Lindsey took with him two more letters of introduction, one to Mr. Foster in Hartford, Connecticut, and the other to the Reverend Dr. Samuel Osgood, in Springfield, Massachusetts.

Again, Lindsey was warmly welcomed upon his arrival in Hartford by Mr. Foster, who took up a collection on his behalf. He then boarded a steamboat for Springfield, Massachusetts, taking with him his next letter of recommendation. He also took a new formal name, James Lindsey Smith, but he continued to go by Lindsey. (James Smith was the name of the plantation owner from whom Zip had run away.)

In Massachusetts Reverend Osgood helped Lindsey find employment as a shoemaker. Lindsey said, "It was the first work that I had ever done in the like of a freeman, which gave me the strength to think I was a man with others." Reverend Osgood also made it possible for Lindsey to attain an education in Wilbraham, Massachusetts, enabling him to run his own business, become a public speaker on the antislavery lecture circuit, and earn a degree as a Methodist minister.

Lindsey married Emeline Minerva Platt in 1842 and settled in Norwich, Connecticut. He eventually bought a home, owned a shoe shop, and educated his four children. In 1845, seven years after settling in Norwich, James Lindsey Smith mistakenly thought he saw an old master in town. He said, "I had determined never to be taken back alive. Death was preferable to slavery, now that I had tasted the sweets of liberty."

In 1867, two years after the Civil War ended slavery, Lindsey returned to Heathsville, Virginia, for a visit. His boat landed at Cone Wharf, the exact spot where he had begun his escape nearly thirty years earlier. He was reunited with friends, two of his sisters, and a brother.

Many of the wealthy slave owners he had known in Virginia were now poor and hungry. Some of the great plantations had been divided and sold to those who were once enslaved. Lindsey accepted an invitation to dine with his former mistress, a twice-widowed woman whom he knew as Mrs. Sarah Langston. It was she who had done nothing, all those years before, to see that his injured leg received proper attention. She was most interested in the tale of his escape and his new life. In appreciation of her acceptance of him as a free man,

Lindsey presented her with a pair of shoes. There had been a time when his former mistress would not walk outside without a slave to hold an umbrella to shade her, but now she was being forced to grow her own subsistence garden under the beating sun.

James Lindsey Smith spent nearly a month visiting the places where he had spent his youth, drinking from springs where his now dispersed family had once gathered. Over the years he would make repeated visits to Heathsville, often arriving with charitable boxes of clothing and necessities donated by the townspeople of Norwich, Connecticut, where he made his home with his wife and children—having never forgotten what it was like to be without.

THE HOUSE ON THE HILL
"Eliza's" River Run

1838

Clumps of white snow fell from the treetops along the Ohio River. In February 1838 the wet ice of the river was peppered with melting potholes. Given a coming thaw, the river moaned with thunderous cracks as the ice broke up.

In Dover, Kentucky, an anonymous slave mother overheard her master talking to a slave trader. Panic ran through her veins. Had she just heard right? Could it be that her master's financial difficulties would prompt him to sell off her two-year-old child? Regardless of the reason, she was determined to make her escape across the Ohio River—that very night.

She had heard about an abolitionist family in Ripley, Ohio, who had built a redbrick house on the highest point above the river. It was clearly visible on a twenty-acre tract of open land. The house boldly displayed a bright lantern at night in defiance to slave owners across the river. Finding that light was the woman's only chance to protect her child.

As soon as night fell, the woman bundled up her baby and ran out into the cold. The hillside on Kentucky's side of the river was so steep that only sheep grazed among the thick tree growth. After a mile and a half, she made her way down to Stony Point, but the ice appeared to be breaking up. Not knowing what to do next, she neared a cabin and ventured to knock on the stranger's door.

Luckily the old white man took her in. He warned her that it was not a good time to cross the river. With the thaw, nobody had dared to walk on the ice for days. Perhaps if she waited till the next night, the river might refreeze. However, that evening in the distance, they both heard the baying of bloodhounds, which could only mean slave catchers were in the area. If it was a choice between risking death on the river ice and being separated from her baby, she would risk death. The man understood. He provided her with a wooden plank from his fence to help her on her crossing. He was certain the ice would break and she would need something to hold on to.

With the hounds drawing close, the woman lurched desperately into the icy water. She leaped onto the nearest ice floe, clasping her baby to her breast with one arm and holding the wooden plank in the other. She crawled onto the unsteady sheet of ice. A bone-chilling wind blew across the half-frozen river, but she had to escape her pursuers who were closing in. She stepped from one ice cake to another. Even those pieces of ice that looked sturdy kept breaking apart beneath her, dropping her into the frigid Ohio River. With each plunge she pushed her baby onto the next frozen chunk and heaved herself up. In the distance, she saw a light high up on a hill.

Swimming, crawling, falling, she forced her frozen limbs forward. Mustering every ounce of her remaining strength, she finally waded through the last feet of frigid water and collapsed on the shore.

But her terrifying and courageous flight across the river hadn't gone unnoticed. The notorious slave catcher Chancey Shaw had been watching from the Ohio side of the river near the mouth of Red Oak Creek. He had braved the cold February night air ever since the river had frozen. His efforts were well rewarded if he caught a runaway—upwards of $500 each. With the recent thaw only desperation would make a slave run the broken river, yet he had heard cries in the night. The moonlight revealed a figure in the dark carrying a screaming child.

As the woman approached the shore, Chancey Shaw saw the slave catchers on the Kentucky side give up and head back up the steep hillside. Shaw approached the woman on the ground and grabbed her arm, thinking only of the reward for capturing a runaway. The desperate woman looked up into his eyes; her baby let out a cry. Never known to have shown compassion to any fugitive, Chancey Shaw now had a change of heart. Maybe this poor woman and her child had earned their chance at freedom after all. He ushered the half-frozen, exhausted woman and hushed baby through town cautiously to avoid being detected. He pointed her to the house on the hill and then disappeared.

The woman looked up the steep hill, still trying to comprehend what had just happened. One hundred rickety steps could be seen in the moonlight, leading to the redbrick house. She saw the beaming lantern and tiredly climbed up. Though the Rankins' dogs had been trained not to bark at runaways, she nervously opened the door to the kitchen. A woman sitting at a warm fire looked up, not at all surprised to see her.

The Rankin family welcomed the woman and her child, feeding them and giving them dry clothes. The slave woman gratefully rocked back and forth with the baby at her breast. As exhausted as the poor woman was, however, it was too dangerous for her and her baby to stay. They needed to be gone before the sun came up. The unnamed woman, though grateful to escape with her baby, shared that she had a grown daughter and grandchildren she was forced to leave behind. She vowed to come back for them someday.

Southerners by birth, abolitionists by inclination, the Reverend John Rankin and his wife, Jean, had moved from the slave states of Tennessee and Kentucky. Their first home in the early 1820s was on Front Street along the Ohio River. In 1829 they built a home overlooking the river. Theirs was one of Ohio's earliest stations on the Underground Railroad, and with a clear view of the Kentucky shore across the river, their light could be seen for miles.

The Rankins had thirteen children and took in another nine. For nearly forty years they gave runaways food, clothing, money, and direction—despite the fact that Reverend Rankin had a $2,500 bounty on his head. Assisting fugitives in the dark of night came to be a way of life for the Rankin children.

Two of the Rankin boys took the fugitive slave woman and her baby to the town of Red Oak, four miles away, showing them to the home of Reverend James Gilliland. The following day they would be forwarded on to Decatur and Sardinia, Ohio. Eventually they would arrive in Newport, Indiana, at the home of Levi Coffin, the "President of the Underground Railroad." From there they would be hurried in and out of various safe houses before finally reaching the safety of Chatham, Canada—more than three hundred miles from the Ohio River.

In 1852 Harriet Beecher Stowe wrote *Uncle Tom's Cabin*. Her legendary character, Eliza Harris, was based on this brave, nameless woman who had crossed Ohio's nearly thawed river in 1838. For fear of incriminating the Rankin family—who could suffer fines, imprisonment, and loss of property if identified—the details of the story were changed. Stowe's "Eliza" was a young, light-skinned woman with a four-year-old son, who was taken in by the owners of a white house in Ripley, Ohio. Her Eliza knew the man on shore who had apprehended her. She also had a husband and had buried two children before fleeing across the half-frozen Ohio River.

The Ripley First Presbyterian Church, where Reverend John Rankin once preached, maintains a vital congregation to this day. Rankin's hilltop house, which operated from 1829 to 1865, was a safe haven for over two thousand runaway slaves. The home is now a National Historic Landmark. Visitors to the Rankin House in Ripley, Ohio, can climb the reconstructed hundred-step stairway to the top of Liberty Hill, the same steps that led so many slaves to freedom.

I HAVE COME BACK
"Eliza" Reappears

1841

John Rankin and his wife, Jean, couldn't have been more surprised while tending their garden in July of 1841. Two figures emerged from a nearby wooded lot, climbed over a fence, and strode through waist-high corn coming toward them. The white man was a stranger, maybe Canadian by his dress. But the black woman looked vaguely familiar. She was five feet, four inches tall and heavyset, not quite middle-aged, and dressed as a man in trousers and a waistcoat. Now Rankin recognized her. It was none other than the brave slave woman who had crossed the icy floes of the Ohio River in February of 1838 with her baby. He had never expected to see her again.

John Rankin's hilltop house above the Ohio River was a known refuge for runaway slaves, a fact that had antagonized slave catchers from Kentucky for years. He had been mobbed more than twenty times, and there was a bounty for his abduction or assassination.

The woman had come back from Canada for her grown daughter and grandchildren, as she had promised herself when she escaped.

They were all slaves on Thomas Davis's farm in Dover, Kentucky, across the Ohio River from the Rankins' house. The French-Canadian man whom she had met in Cleveland along the Underground Railroad route to Canada had agreed to help her, so she hired him to rescue her family. The woman's plan was for the two of them to secretly alert her daughter to be ready and find a boat to take them across the Ohio River. They needed the Rankins' network of connections in order to make their way along the Underground Railroad and back to Canada.

Reverend Rankin found the woman's rescue plan too risky, and strongly advised against it. Her daughter had four sons and three daughters, including a sixteen-month-old, whose cries could betray them. It was a large number to rescue at one time unnoticed. Seeing her determination, however, he eventually agreed to assist her on his side of the river, but she would have to get them first. It would take the cooperation of many agents for the undertaking to be successful.

Work was found for the woman in Red Oak at the Archibald Hopkins farm, just four miles to the north, so she could earn her keep while their plan was set into action. Meanwhile, her accomplice rowed across the Ohio River and found his way to the woman's enslaved family.

The Canadian had no accent, having lived in many places, and blended in well in Dover. Mrs. Rankin had found him clothes suitable to a common laborer. He found a job chopping wood on the Davis farm, where the woman's family lived. He wisely frequented the local taverns and spent time on the riverfront to learn the schedule of the patrollers. Typically they went off duty by 4:00 a.m. and were usually inebriated at that point. He also scouted the shoreline to find a safe departure point that did not have barking dogs that might awaken neighbors.

By the first week of August, all was ready. Late on a Friday night, Rankin's sons, aged eighteen and fifteen, rode horses to the Hopkins farm to pick up the woman. When they returned, the Canadian man was waiting on the riverbank along Front Street. The boys noiselessly rowed the woman and the Canadian across the Ohio River and dropped them off on the Kentucky shore. The escape was to take place the following night.

The woman's daughter took six of her children, leaving behind the eldest daughter, a house servant, to whom they could not get word of the escape plan. Managing the removal of all these people, as well as the couple hundred pounds of belongings her daughter insisted she needed, retarded their progress along the three and a half miles through wooded hills to the river. Despite their best efforts, they could not make it across the river before daylight. The fugitives were forced to hide out on the Kentucky shore on Sunday, hoping to attempt their escape the following night. They took refuge among the thickly timbered land of a farmer named Mike Sullivan.

Sunday morning Davis awoke to find his slaves missing. He organized a posse of a dozen men. The Canadian had stolen Sullivan's skiff before the sun rose and rowed it across to the Ohio side, leaving it prominently displayed to throw off the hunt. The posse crossed the river and spent the entire day searching through the town of Ripley, looking for fugitives they assumed had escaped on Sullivan's skiff, but ironically hadn't even left Kentucky yet.

A $400 reward was immediately offered for information on the whereabouts of Davis's slaves, but the machinery of the Underground Railroad had already begun to turn. The taverns in Ripley, for instance, sold the bounty hunters ale at low prices, hoping to incapacitate them. The Rankin family went to church, knowing that their house would be searched while they were gone.

Around 3:00 a.m. on Monday, the Canadian borrowed an aboli-tionist's boat and rowed from Ohio back to Kentucky, gathering the fugitives and some of their possessions. After dropping his passengers off in Ripley at 5:00 a.m., the Canadian collected his pay and left. His work was done, and he did not want to be implicated in the escape. Two underground agents brought the fugitives up the shore to the home of Thomas and Kitty McCague, wealthy, well-connected Ripley residents. Since the McCagues had slave-owning friends and family in Kentucky, nobody suspected them of being in collusion with the Underground Railroad.

After the search died down, the fugitives were escorted one at a time to the Rankins' house. Once again the unnamed woman sat in the Rankins' kitchen, just as she had done three years earlier, half frozen from her icy crossing. This time she was surrounded by most of her family, and it was a warm summer evening. However, there was no time to grow comfortable.

From the Rankins' house the former slaves traveled to the Hop-kins's farm four miles down the road. Next they were all concealed in a peddler's wagon and were escorted to Hillsboro, Ohio, thirty-five miles to the north. From there they went on to Cleveland, then to Lake Erie, and finally to Canada.

John and Jean Rankin neither saw nor heard from the deter-mined woman and her family again, but were informed of their safe arrival in Canada—adding to the growing number of fugitive slaves who had successfully passed through the Rankins' house on their way to freedom.

THE TWELVE-YEAR MISTAKE
Solomon Northup's Ordeal

1841

Solomon Northup held his aching head in his hands as he winced in pain. Fragmented visions of the previous night floated in his mind: two men, dinner and draught at a tavern, the sudden onset of feeling ill. Then visions of Solomon's hometown of Sarasota Springs, New York, came to mind: images of his wife and family, the hack he drove for the hotel, his carpentry work, playing his violin for his three children. Suddenly an intense shooting pain brought Solomon slowly to consciousness. The weight and the sound of clinking chains fully awakened him.

A sliver of light came from a barred window high on the wall, barely illuminating a sole wooden bench in the small room. He sat up abruptly and adjusted his eyes to the dark. The dank smell indicated he was below ground. Solomon was chained in shackles and caged up like an animal in a dungeon. This was no dream from his bed in Sarasota Springs—it was the beginning of a nightmare.

Solomon Northup tried to piece together the chain of events that had led him, a free black citizen of New York, to this barren cell.

Though his head was pounding, he vaguely recalled meeting two affable men on the corner of Congress Street and Broadway in Sarasota Springs—Merrill Brown and Abram Hamilton. They were associated with a traveling circus from Washington, DC, and had praised his skills as a fiddler. Unfortunately, Solomon had agreed to provide musical accompaniment for their acts.

Sarasota Springs, New York, was a resort town located in the foothills of the Adirondack Mountains where people came for the cool mineral spring waters and their healing effects. Both Northup and his wife, Anne, worked at the United States Hotel. She was a cook and Solomon drove a hack among other part-time jobs. Due to a lull in the tourist season that March of 1841, Solomon agreed to take the part-time job with the two strangers. He regretted not leaving his family a note before he departed.

Solomon berated himself for taking up with these unknown villains who had surely tricked him. His stomach wrenched with fear: Had he been kidnapped and sold into slavery? The thought seemed preposterous, yet it was common knowledge that free black citizens in the North were kidnapped off the streets and sold into slavery. Solomon and his family lived a comfortable and respectable life, never once imagining such horror. He regrettably had become complacent.

Brown and Hamilton seemed trustworthy and had paid Solomon handsomely, so he accompanied his abductors to New York City. After asking Solomon to continue with them to Washington, DC, they even took him to get free papers in case his free status was ever questioned. After that, Solomon's recollections became fuzzy.

Just then the lock of Solomon's cell opened and two repugnant-looking men walked in. Solomon soon learned that James H. Birch and Ebenezer Radburn were slave dealers. Birch asked his prisoner how he felt, and an indignant Solomon Northup stated his name, insisted he was a free man from Saratoga Springs, New York, and told them a terrible misunderstanding had taken place. Birch angrily responded that Solomon was a runaway slave from Georgia whom he had bought and was sending to New Orleans. Solomon could barely comprehend what the man said and vehemently protested.

Immediately Solomon was stripped of his clothes and his dignity. He was then thrown over a wooden bench, where Radburn held him down with his foot on the wrist chain and shackles. Birch took a thick paddle with holes bored into it and beat Solomon mercilessly blow after blow, repeatedly asking him if he was a free man. A proud and stubborn Northup insisted it was true despite the cruel flogging.

His tormentor eventually switched to a knotted rope with cat-o'-nine-tails, whipping him like a madman and tearing the flesh off Solomon's back. Through the fiery pain Solomon would not give up his insistence that he was a free man. An irate Birch stopped lashing him for fear of killing Solomon and wasting the money he had spent purchasing his piece of property. This newly initiated slave might bring him $1,000.

With blistering pain of both body and soul, Solomon realized his awful yet incomprehensible fate and wept bitterly. He was completely overcome with feelings of betrayal, despair, and hopelessness. He was a thirty-three-year-old free man. His father had been freed upon the death of his master when he was twenty years old. His mother was free. Solomon's wife and children were free.

Solomon was soon confined in William's Slave Pen in Washington, DC. After a few days he was let out into a yard where he met other slaves in the same predicament as his. Though not knowing it at the time, one of the men, Clemens Ray, would play a part in Northup's eventual release years later.

Ray was to be sold down south in New Orleans. Another man in the yard had been abducted from his master in an attempt to collect a debt. His master arrived, paid up, and reclaimed his slave property. A refined black woman and her two children had been brought to the city under false pretenses of being liberated, yet instead were sold to a slave trader. Thus was Solomon's indoctrination into the grim and illegal slave trade business that operated beneath the eyes of his nation's sleeping capital.

Solomon Northup's journey began in upstate New York and ended in Bayou Beouf, the marshy river outlet in central Louisiana below the lower Red River. Solomon quickly learned to lose any appearance of intelligence in speech or manner and never reveal that he could read and write for fear of death. Instead he took off his hat and had downcast eyes when talking to any master, of which he had several during his twelve years in bondage laboring on cotton and sugarcane plantations.

A glimmer of hope came aboard the brig *Orleans* on his way to New Orleans. An English sailor named John Manning took pity on Solomon after hearing his plight and secreted a letter from Solomon to an attorney in Sandy Hill, New York, named Henry B. Northup, whom Solomon had known as a child.

Upon arriving in New Orleans, Solomon was given the name of Platt, examined like a common animal, and sold for $900 to William Ford. Reverend Ford was a Baptist minister of Rapides Parish who operated a sawmill in the heart of Louisiana swampland. He proved to be a good master, but one of Ford's men, named Tibaut, had it out for Northup. The man whipped Solomon without cause, attempted to hang him, and came after him with a hatchet, whereupon Northup fled. Solomon outran Tibaut's pack of dogs and waded through an alligator- and snake-infested Cocodrie Swamp before circling back to the plantation. Reverend Ford sold Solomon, knowing the evil-minded Tibaut would kill him otherwise.

Solomon Northup's worst nightmare was realized when he came to his third owner, Edwin Epps, in 1843. Epps owned a three-hundred-acre cotton plantation on Bayou Beouf (near Holmesville) in central Louisiana. Driven by narrow profit margins and poor temperament, Epps took his frustrations out on his slaves. He proved to be barbaric—the vilest excuse of a man Northup had ever met. He rode horseback through the cotton fields, cracking his whip upon the backs of his Negro laborers, especially if their pickings did not exceed the previous day's take. When Epps took to drink he sunk to even lower levels of brutality, ruthlessly whipping his slaves without provocation.

Master Epps turned his affections to a young slave Solomon befriended named Patsey, which incensed Epps's hateful, insanely jealous wife. Patsey was often whipped to within an inch of her life. Solomon suffered the mental anguish of being forced to partake in whippings, yet he was often the recipient of countless cruel floggings himself.

In 1852 an antislavery Canadian carpenter named Samuel Bass came to work on Epps's plantation. A desperate Solomon debated risking his life in seeking Bass's empathy. Previous mistrusted attempts had nearly gotten him killed. Northup approached Bass and explained his plight, which ultimately set the wheels in motion for his release from bondage.

Bass carried a letter written by Solomon on August 15 as well as letters Bass himself wrote. The letters implored judges and important connections in Saratoga Springs, New York, and the surrounding area to inquire about Solomon's free status and secure free papers as proof.

At daybreak on January 3, 1853, a carriage arrived at Epps's plantation with two distinguished-looking white gentlemen. One was the sheriff from Avoyelles Parish in Louisiana, and the other was Henry B. Northup, the lawyer from New York whom Solomon had known since childhood, the very man the English sailor on the brig

Orleans had secreted a letter years earlier. Henry B. Northup's great uncle, Captain Henry Northup, had owned Solomon's father, Mintus Northup, hence they shared the same surname.

Henry B. Northup was an agent of New York's governor, ironically named Washington Hunt, who was authorized to search out and return free black citizens that had been kidnapped into slavery. In the lawyer's possession were letters proving Solomon Northup's free status from his wife, a senator, a Supreme Court justice, and acquaintances, all vouching for Solomon.

An incensed Master Epps was informed of the situation and shown the appropriate papers proving "Platt" was indeed Solomon Northup, a free man from New York. Over the years Solomon's hopes of attaining freedom had risen and fallen. Just two days prior, he had received fifteen lashes from Master Epps's whip for oversleeping, yet unbelievably here he was about to have his free status proven.

Solomon's kidnappers, the men who had convinced Solomon to come away with them, Merrill Brown and Abram Hamilton, were actually named Alexander Merrill and Joseph Russell. They, along with the men who sold him into slavery, James H. Birch and Ebenezer Radburn, were arrested and brought to trial. However, the legal system in Washington, DC, and New York failed Solomon Northup: All were acquitted, and Solomon himself was disallowed from testifying because he was black.

On January 22, 1853, forty-six-year-old Solomon Northup, after twelve years of enslavement, was reunited with his wife, Anne, and his children, Elizabeth, Margaret, and Alonzo, who were aged ten, eight, and five when their father was kidnapped. It was a surreal reunion for everyone.

Solomon Northup learned that Clemens Ray, the slave he had met years ago in the yard in William's Slave Pen in Washington, DC, had gotten word to Northup's family. Clemens had managed to escape, and on his journey to Canada's free soil, he happened to stay at the safe house of Solomon's brother-in-law in Saratoga, whereupon he informed Solomon's family of his kidnapping and enslavement. Solomon's letter to Henry B. Northup, which was carried by John Manning, the sailor from the brig *Orleans*, had also arrived—but Solomon was unreachable in such a remote and isolated area, lost in the bowels of Louisiana.

The same year Solomon was freed, he wrote and published a book titled *Twelve Years a Slave*. It became a bestseller, with eight thousand copies sold the first month. Solomon worked to aid the abolishment of slavery by speaking on the antislavery lecture circuit around the North, as well as starring in theatrical performances about his enslavement and rescue. He also became an active participant in the Underground Railroad, aiding fugitives' escapes from Vermont to Canada. He gave generously, giving what little money he had to the cause.

Solomon Northup was last mentioned in a newspaper in 1857, but no public records give an account of him after the mid-1860s, leaving his death a mystery. There is speculation that his captors re-enslaved him, that he changed his name and worked anonymously with the clandestine Underground Railroad, or that he died of unknown causes in an unknown region.

Interest in Solomon Northup's story continues to this day. His journey can be traced along an established Northup Trail, which begins at the Louisiana State University in Alexandria on through Rapides and Avoyelles Parishes, where visitors can tour various plantations on which Solomon labored.

In 1999 Saratoga Springs, New York, began hosting the annual Solomon Northup Day—A Celebration of Freedom, now run by Skidmore College. Descendants of Solomon Northup have attended the event over the years, including his great-granddaughter, Victoria Northup Linzy Dunham, who lived to age ninety-eight. Descendants of those who were instrumental in Northup's release, such as the Canadian-born abolitionist-minded Samuel Bass, have also come to honor him. It was Solomon Northup's great-great-granddaughter who astutely stated that Northup's astonishing saga teaches us all "about persistence and determination in the face of extraordinary adversity."

A WOLF IN SHEEP'S CLOTHES
Laura Smith Haviland
and the Slave Catchers

1846

Willis Hamilton of Jonesborough, Tennessee, didn't know what surprised him more—the fact that his owner, Deacon John Bayliss, had been challenged, or that he actually listened. The old slave, Aunt Lucy, dared to question how exactly his sermon on the Golden Rule applied to slaves: Do unto others as you would have them do unto you. Regardless, Aunt Lucy had raised the deacon's moral consciousness, which resulted in his manumitting all twenty of his slaves. So it was that in 1843 Willis Hamilton became a free man.

Three years later, Willis learned that his wife, Elsie, who belonged to a neighboring planter, was going to be sold farther south. A distraught Willis implored everyone he knew to purchase Elsie for him. A man named John P. Chester bought Elsie for $800, with the understanding that Willis would contribute $300 of labor to assist with her purchase price.

A few months later, however, Elsie got wind of Chester's plan to sell both her and her husband downriver to New Orleans for a nice profit, disregarding the fact that Willis was a free man. Willis and Elsie Hamilton sought the advice of Deacon Bayliss. He advised the Hamiltons to assume new identities and go north. They would have to leave their two daughters behind for now and come back for them later.

The distraught parents were forwarded on the Underground Railroad to a Quaker community in Indiana. After a year they went briefly to Canada and then returned to the States, settling in Michigan. Good fortune smiled on them when they leased land on a farm in Adrian, Michigan, from Laura Smith Haviland—the woman who had organized the first Anti-slavery Society in Michigan. The petite, unassuming abolitionist was not easily intimidated—even when Elsie Hamilton's owner would later point a pistol at Haviland's head.

In 1846 Willis Hamilton had a letter written to his former master, Deacon Bayliss, inquiring about the whereabouts of his and Elsie's two daughters. Little did they know that letter never reached him.

They did, however, receive a reply. John P. Chester, who had bought Elsie Hamilton and to whom Willis owed $300, intercepted the letter. Chester was serving as postmaster in Jonesborough, Tennessee. He suspected the letter from Michigan directed to Deacon Bayliss might be from the Hamiltons, and upon opening the letter, he was proved right.

Chester wanted his slave property back. Together with his son, Thomas, and a son-in-law, they concocted a plan to trick the Hamiltons and recapture them. Chester wrote several letters to the Hamiltons, purporting to be Deacon Bayliss. The first letter reported that the girls were well, and he was eager to see Willis and Elsie. He wanted to know where they lived and even sent money, imploring them to come for a visit.

When another letter from Deacon Bayliss arrived, claiming that he had fallen ill on a trip to Toledo, Ohio, and begging them to come see him, Mrs. Haviland refused to write a response, finding it all suspicious. But Willis and Elsie desperately wanted to reclaim their daughters and insisted on visiting the sickly deacon who had befriended them years earlier. Fearing it was a trap, Mrs. Haviland instead decided that a free black man named James Martin, who resembled Willis in appearance, would go see the infirm deacon in Willis's place to relay a message. Mrs. Haviland and her seventeen-year-old son would accompany Martin. The three traveled to Toledo and stayed at the Indiana House, a fine hotel friendly to abolitionists.

Upon arriving at the nearby Toledo Hotel, James Martin asked to see the ailing deacon up in his room. When Elsie's old master, John P. Chester, his son Thomas, and the son-in-law realized that the black man was not Willis Hamilton, they put down their guns and attempted to bribe Martin into helping them capture the Hamiltons, but to no avail. So the three slave catchers devised another plan.

Before James Martin was released downstairs, Laura Smith Haviland was summoned to another room. Thomas Chester was lying in bed, pretending to be the ailing Deacon Bayliss. John P. Chester played the part of the deacon's doctor. The doctor said his patient "Deacon Bayliss" was suffering from bilious fever and typhus. His dying wish was to see the Hamiltons once more. The doctor implored Mrs. Haviland to bring them to Toledo at once, but she was not fooled by the plan.

According to Willis Hamilton, his former master, Deacon Bayliss, was short and rather portly. The patient in front of her now was thin and over six feet tall. Though his face was covered in bandages, it seemed to be long and angular rather than round. A bin of vomited bile conspicuously placed near his bed looked to be a mixture of coffee grounds and ink with a spattering of spittle. Upon examination she could feel for herself that the deacon had a normal temperature and a healthy pulse.

Yet Mrs. Haviland acted as if she was convinced poor Deacon Bayliss was indeed on his death bed. Fearing for her own safety, she agreed to go back to Michigan and return with the Hamilton family on the next train. Instead, the doctor insisted they all stay in Toledo and she write a letter to the Hamiltons ordering them to come immediately. A porter stood by to deliver the letter.

The "doctor" dictated a letter to her. When they were finished, Mrs. Haviland requested to add a few additional lines of her own, advising Elsie to borrow some traveling clothes for herself and the children. The doctor agreed to the postscript: "Tell Elsie to take for herself the black alpaca dress in the south bed-room, and the two pink gingham aprons and striped flannel dresses in the bureau in the west room for the little girls. To come to Toledo, take the double team farm wagon." None of these items existed—Mrs. Haviland hoped Elsie would know the letter was a lie.

The next morning Mrs. Haviland, her son, and James Martin boarded the 8:00 a.m. train to Adrian, Michigan. The Chesters were also on the train, planning to meet up with the porter they had dispatched with the letter to apprehend the Hamiltons. Perhaps the Chesters felt that they had outsmarted Laura Smith Haviland. When the passengers briefly detrained in Sylvania, Ohio, a small farming community ten miles west of Toledo, they approached her with drawn guns, threatening her and calling her names such as "damned nigger stealer."

Mrs. Haviland was not intimidated, as she was in abolitionist-friendly territory. Fugitive slaves were often rerouted through Sylvania whenever the Underground Railroad through Toledo was deemed unsafe. The back roads near the Lathrop and Harroun farms were off the beaten track, and fugitives were secreted over the ravine between the two houses. Sylvania's abolitionists, who often went so far as to risk hiding fugitives in a concealed room in the Lathrop basement behind a fake oven, would never let the Chesters bring kidnapped fugitive slaves back on the train through their town.

The train conductor, who witnessed the Chesters threatening an elderly woman with a gun, was about to have the men arrested. However, when the Chesters realized they were clearly outnumbered by a mob of irate abolitionists, they fled. Word of the incident spread, and the Sylvania townspeople promised to tear up the track if it were discovered that the Hamiltons were being taken against their will on a southbound train.

Back home in Michigan, Willis and Elsie Hamilton knew that Mrs. Haviland's letter delivered by the hotel porter was a hoax, since she did not own either the clothes or the team of horses mentioned in the postscript. The porter was clearly frustrated by his inability to convince Willis and Elsie to come with him, and had to leave empty-handed.

The Chesters were enraged at being outwitted. They sent a series of threatening letters to Laura Smith Haviland and offered a $3,000 reward for her capture, which did nothing to deter her abolitionist work. Within six months of the ordeal, Willis and Elsie Hamilton and their four children had moved to Canada, never having been reunited with the two daughters they'd left in Tennessee.

Three years later, empowered by the Fugitive Slave Act of 1850, the Chesters set out to capture the Hamiltons once again, but failed. John P. Chester was later shot through the heart when he attempted to remand a mulatto man into slavery after insisting that his free papers were fake. Chester's son, Thomas, who had impersonated the ill Deacon Bayliss, died a horrible death from yellow fever some months later.

Laura Smith Haviland helped found an interracial school, the Raisin Institute. She established homes for orphans and served as a nurse in the Civil War. She worked for the Freedman's Aid Bureau, was involved in the temperance movement, and fought for women's right to vote. The petite, Canadian-born Quaker woman and mother of seven children whose size belied her strength and resolve also would not let herself be outwitted by slave catchers.

MY BETTER HALF
Tom and Liz's Big Fight

1847

After almost one entire year of freedom up North, "George" walked one hundred miles south, back into slave territory. As soon as he crossed the border, he took up his former name, Tom, and sneaked into his wife's slave quarters after dark. He put his hand over her mouth so she would not scream as she awoke. Liz almost fainted at the sight of her husband. Releasing his hand from her mouth, he whispered in her ear, "I tell you, Liz, I ain't got whole freedom without you." Tom quickly outlined his plan to ask his master to take him back, feigning he was sick of freedom, and then vanished back into the night.

One year earlier, in the autumn of 1846, Tom and his friend Jim had escaped north, briefly hiding in the basement of the Zion Baptist Church in Cincinnati, Ohio. A white woman named Laura Smith Haviland, also known as "Aunt Laura," saw that they were fed and clothed. Tom dressed in linen pants, a blue-checked gingham coat, and a straw hat. Jim donned thin pants and a palm-leaf hat. The fugitives took new names to further conceal their identities and were secreted to another safe house. Mrs. Haviland made arrangements for them to be taken on to a Quaker community eighty miles farther north. She never expected to see either of them again.

Jim continued on to Canada, but Tom remained among the Quakers, finding work and saving his wages. He continued to wear the clothes he had run away in, patching them over and over until they were near rags. No one knew of his plans to return to slavery. Nearly twelve months after his escape, Tom stole away in the dark of night, returning to Kentucky.

The morning after visiting Liz, Tom walked eight miles to his old master's house, wearing the tattered clothes he had run away in. Master Carpenter was shocked to see him return to his plantation but even more stunned when Tom spoke.

With a big grin Tom told his former master that he was happy to be back and that he never wanted to leave again. He claimed that the free black man was overworked and underpaid in the North. He told of how he never was given any new clothes and never had enough to eat. Tom shook his head and said, "Abolitioners the greates' rascals I ever seen. I wants no more ov' em. They tried hard to git me to Canada; but I got all I wants of Canada. An' I tell you, Massa Carpenter, all I wants is one good stiddy home." Then Tom fished the crumpled $80 he'd earned out of his pocket, and with an outstretched arm, he said, "I don't want this money; it's yourn."

Master Carpenter was shocked but pleased to see his former slave and welcomed Tom back. Carpenter bragged of Tom's return to the neighboring planters, explaining that apparently Tom had left on account of a big fight with his wife. It was clear Tom hated Liz, but he wanted to come back home. Carpenter told them, "He came back perfectly disgusted with abolitionists; he said they will work a fellow half to death for low wages." Even so, the other masters found it hard to trust a runaway who had sampled a taste of freedom. Tom was warned that if he stepped onto his wife's plantation, he would be shot. This gave Master Carpenter a good laugh, claiming, "You couldn't hire Tom to go near Liz."

Tom became as dedicated and trustworthy a slave as there ever was. At first Lizzie's master had a bloodhound trained to keep Tom off his property, fearing he might come for her. After a couple months, however, her master became convinced of Liz's disgust with Tom, and he returned the hound to its owner and let his guard down.

After three months Master Carpenter's friends had heard enough good things about Tom being obedient, hardworking, and content to be back that they had no objections when Carpenter allowed him to attend slave gatherings on neighboring plantations. They even thought it might be a good deterrent if their slaves heard about the evils of freedom and how abolitionists "pretend to be your friends, but they were your worst enemies."

Tom appeared uninterested in joining with the other slaves who were socializing, singing, and praying, so Master Carpenter had to urge him to go. Tom insisted on only attending day meetings so the owners could keep an eye on him. He was overheard telling other slaves how awful it was up North.

One day Liz raised a fuss about possessions Tom had left in her cabin when he ran away. She made it known that she meant to burn them or pitch them to the pigs if he did not claim them soon. She wanted no reminder of a man who left her to chase a foolhardy dream that turned out bad. Word was sent to Tom to come to the meeting the following week for his things.

Tom's master instructed him to retrieve his clothes, perhaps so that he would not have to spend money replacing them. Tom dutifully obeyed and made his way to Lizzie's plantation. Seeing Liz, he caused a huge scene by hurling insults at her. She retorted with name-calling and said that his leaving did nothing to make her feel bad and she didn't care if she ever saw him again. The two raised a ruckus, with Liz yelling how she didn't care he had left and Tom hollering how he never liked her anyway. Tom's feelings were clear: "I never wanted to see her face agin, an' we almos' come to blows."

Tom and Liz's act convinced others of their hatred for each other. Secretly they saw each other infrequently and communicated only through a trusted messenger. Several months later, the second phase of the plan was ready.

A holiday was approaching and Tom, who wished to visit his aunt, had no problem getting a pass from Master Carpenter. Like-wise, Lizzie received a pass from her master to go see friends. The night before they were to leave, Tom snuck onto Liz's plantation. Again he covered her mouth so as not to startle her and laid out the details of their rendezvous. The next day after sundown, they both left their respective plantations, with Tom heading six miles in one direction and Liz walking five miles the other way.

They walked until it was dark. Then they each turned toward the Licking River in Kentucky, one of them walking upriver and the other downriver until they met. Away from the watchful eyes of plan-tation owners, they were free to embrace and speak lovingly to each other before quickly carrying out the third phase of the plan.

Tom searched the riverbank for a usable skiff. This took some time, since boats were often secured to the shore without oars, ren-dering them useless to possible runaways. After finding a small boat with oars, they jumped in, and Tom rowed off in darkness, pulling north for the Ohio River.

At daybreak they hid the skiff in the brush near the river's edge, hiding the oars in some undergrowth to retrieve later. Tom and Liz found cover farther inland in a thicket. They felt safe until some mis-chievous boys stumbled across their skiff, using poles to propel it off the bank for a joyride. It was a close call for Tom and Liz, who had almost been ferreted out while the boys searched for the missing oars.

After nightfall Tom and Liz explored the riverbank for a suitable skiff. Near midnight they found one. Once again Tom rowed hard until close to daybreak, when at last they approached the junction of the Ohio River.

Just when they thought their bondage was a thing of the past, two men beside the Licking River spotted them. They yelled out, asking where Tom and Liz were headed. Tom replied that they were going to market. The men seemed suspicious and inquired what they were carrying in their boat to sell. Tom replied they had butter and eggs and bid them farewell. The men began making their way to a boat at the water's edge, and at that moment Tom knew he was in for the race of his life.

Forgoing polite conversation, Tom turned his skiff for Ohio's shoreline and took off, heaving at the oars with every ounce of strength he had. Even with freedom in sight, both Tom and Liz knew that if they were caught, it would likely lead to a fate worse than death. Neither of their masters would take being fooled lightly.

Tom gasped for breath, sweat dripping off his flushed face, and his aching muscles burned as if they were on fire. Halfway across the Ohio River, he nervously glanced behind him to see how close his pursuers were. Apparently, when the men had seen that they would not be able to catch Tom and Liz, they had turned back—luckily they were not armed. Tom felt physically and emotionally drained but was thankful that he and Liz were out of immediate danger.

Once ashore, Tom led Liz to the Zion Baptist Church that had sheltered him the year before. They hid in the basement until Laura Smith Haviland came to see to their needs. Tom remembered Aunt Laura immediately and was quite excited to see her. Mrs. Haviland, in meeting so many fugitives, could not place him at first. Tom replied that he was none other than the man "George" who had come through last summer. He reminded her that she had given him the linen pants, blue-checked gingham coat, and straw hat that she had pulled from her large market basket. Mrs. Haviland remembered having arranged for the two men to be taken in a wagon to a Quaker community. When she asked how he came to pass through again, Tom replied, "It was for this little woman I went back."

Tom and Liz, renamed George and Mary, joined other fugitives that Laura Smith Haviland was conducting along the Underground Railroad through Toledo and then to Detroit and finally on to the safe haven of Canada.

There is no account of how Tom's and Lizzie's masters took the news of their escape. Master Carpenter was surely dumbfounded, if not embarrassed. And it must have brought a smile to Tom's face knowing that, through his fine acting, he had outwitted the lot of them. Apparently, he had wanted something to do with Canada after all.

READING THE STARS
Barney Ford, Civil Rights Pioneer

1847

Barney turned and looked at the reflection in the mirror. There stood the slight form of a twenty-five-year-old woman dressed in a blue gown and cape with long white gloves. Her head was adorned with a frilly bonnet. Lace encircled her face. Her eyes, a combination of hazel and blue, peered out from a complexion of white and pink powdered greasepaint. The transformation was unbelievable, but Barney couldn't help but worry what kind of punishment he might receive if he were caught impersonating a white woman.

Barney was born in Virginia on the plantation of Charles S. Darlington, his master and biological father. His mother, Phoebe, had drowned when he was fourteen while trying to make contact with someone who was going to help facilitate an escape. Barney was not about to let his mother's dream for him to run away and get an education go down with her.

In 1836 Matt Bartlett bought Barney for his brother-in-law, James Fenstanton, but was allowed to keep him as long as needed.

Bartlett, a hog and cattle trader, traveled considerable distances transporting his animals. On their long journeys to market together, he read aloud and Barney gained an education about the world.

After three years Barney was sent back to the Fenstantons near Columbus, Georgia, along the Chattahoochee River. Mistress Fenstanton took a liking to him and encouraged Barney to continue learning to read and write by secretly allowing him the use of Master Fenstanton's library. His education improved a great deal in his seven years with the Fenstantons, but he was warned never to reveal he could read or write, as it was against the law.

In 1846, when Barney was twenty-four years old, his owners moved to Saint Louis, Missouri. Barney was hired out to work on the Mississippi steamboat *Magnolia Blossom*. The expansive riverboat was something to behold, with its glass-enclosed deck, giant paddle wheel, and powerful steam engine. It traveled from Louisville, Kentucky, down the Ohio River to the Mississippi, all the way to New Orleans then back again. Barney saw more sights than he had ever imagined possible.

While working on the *Magnolia Blossom*, Barney was befriended by a British Shakespearean actor named J. Anthony Preston, who entertained on board. Preston realized Barney had great potential and thought he would do well if he ever escaped. He told Barney about abolitionists who opposed slavery, and he gave Barney Northern newspapers to read.

About a year later, Master Fenstanton decided Barney's time on the *Magnolia Blossom* was over. He wanted him back on the plantation in Georgia. Barney thought about his mother's dream—freedom and education for her son. Barney trusted J. Anthony Preston with that dream and told him he wanted to be free. Preston realized Barney would never have a better chance to escape than when the riverboat was docked on the Mississippi River next to a free state.

Preston taught Barney how to read the stars by always looking for the North Star, which served as a guide to Canada. He outlined the Big Dipper (also referred to as the "drinking gourd") as a picture in the night sky. He showed Barney the two stars on the Dipper's edge that pointed to the North Star, which never changed position. He explained how fugitive slaves used other signs to aid them heading north: to look for moss growing on the north side of trees, and to notice the northerly direction birds migrated during the summer.

Barney also learned about the workings of the Underground Railroad in Quincy, Illinois, but beyond that area Preston did not know who Barney could trust. He warned him to rely on his instincts about whom he should approach along the way. Preston told him local people wearing red handkerchiefs were the ones who could help forward him on, and he gave Barney the code words to use that would help him meet up with his contacts.

As Preston applied his stage makeup for his nightly show in his dressing room, he stared in the mirror. That's when he arrived at the idea of dressing Barney up as a woman. Applying stage makeup on Barney would be easier due to the advantage of his light eyes and skin.

The next morning after Barney finished serving breakfast, he snuck into the actor's dressing room. Preston got to work disguising Barney as "Miss Cora May." Then he had to wake Barney from the trance he had fallen into while staring at himself in the dressing room mirror. The *Magnolia Blossom* had docked at Quincy, Illinois, and it was time to depart. As they left the dressing room, J. Anthony Preston was engaged in a lively conversation with the charming young Miss Cora May, who held his arm and hung on his every word.

It was a cacophony of noise and confusion on the deck of the *Magnolia Blossom*. Bells rang above the splashing water from the great paddle wheel. Deckhands yelled directions as they unloaded crates. Hovering seagulls squawked overhead. Outwardly calm but inwardly terrified, Barney sashayed down the gangplank on the arm of Mr. Preston. His heart briefly stopped when the ship's captain came toward them, but the captain only nodded good day to the actor and then passed by—taking no notice of Miss Cora May.

Preston found a carriage for hire, gave the password to the driver, and assisted Miss Cora May inside. He kissed Cora May's gloved hand and watched as her fluttering handkerchief waved good-bye from the window. Tears of joy would have ruined his makeup, so Barney composed himself as the carriage took him away on the Underground Railroad.

His first stop was a barn. Inside, Barney was given a chance to clean up and put on men's clothing. The costume dress and wig were packed to be returned to the actor. Barney hid in the hayloft until evening, at which time he was put in a wagon and covered with straw. He traveled until daybreak, and then once again was hidden in a barn loft. The plan was to forward him to Peoria, Illinois, but word had it that slave hunters and their bloodhounds were scouring the area, looking for runaways.

To avoid capture, Barney's conductor backtracked. While this seemed counterproductive, Barney realized that he had no other choice but to trust those who were helping him. Barney was given falsified papers stating his owner in Alabama had given him manumission and he was free.

Barney boarded a boat going south on the Illinois River. He worked on the boat as directed, loading and unloading crates. After several days a farmhand wearing a red handkerchief came by to hire some men. He asked Barney in code, "Who's your friend?" Barney replied, "The North Star is my friend," and the contact took him on.

Barney was informed that his escape from the *Magnolia Blossom* had been discovered and an advertisement for his capture had been circulating. Now it was necessary to be forwarded north along an alternate route. He was pointed to a town and told to knock on the door of a certain doctor's office. He was then whisked to a nearby cellar, where he spent the day. That evening he was hidden in a wagon that took him to a funeral home. Barney was put inside a casket with small air holes and driven forty miles. He was let out, given some cursory directions and signposts, and told that he was to follow the North Star to a town called Vandalia.

Barney traveled at night and hid during the day in fields or woods. When he heard dogs barking in the distance, his heart raced and the hair stood up on his neck. At one point he narrowly escaped a group of patrollers. Muddy, thirsty, hungry, and exhausted, he braved all sorts of weather and walked a seemingly endless number of miles. At times he found churches that offered him food, and at other times he went hungry. But always, he kept the North Star as his compass.

In what would become Kankakee, Illinois, Barney searched for a certain church he'd been told about. He found his next contact and was hidden in the church's belfry and given food. A few days later he was transported out of town in the false bottom of a vegetable wagon. Barney completed his circuitous route to freedom and arrived safely in Chicago, Illinois, having been delivered to a livery stable.

Barney became friends with the owner of the livery, H. O. Wagoner, and began working with him on the Underground Railroad, assisting many fugitive slaves. In 1849 at the age of twenty-seven, he married Wagoner's sister-in-law, Julia Lyoni. She had asked Barney to take a surname, as all freemen had, and suggested Lancelot Ford, after a popular railroad steam engine of the day.

Barney L. Ford was destined for success. In 1851 he and his wife set out for the California gold fields by ship. However, when they reached Central America, Barney decided to stay in Nicaragua. He purchased and managed several hotels and restaurants, which turned out to be a successful enterprise. However, political unrest in Nicaragua prompted the couple's return to Chicago. Barney Ford bought a livery stable and assisted with the Underground Railroad once again.

Barney was then lured west by the Pike's Peak Gold Rush in 1860. At age thirty-eight he went to Colorado to try his luck. After he was cheated out of his mining profits by a claim jumper, Barney brought his wife and three children to Denver and began a career as a barber and small restaurateur. His business and much of Denver were burned in the great fire of 1863, but Barney borrowed money to rebuild. He became a prominent restaurateur, caterer, and hotelier whose businesses were frequented by presidents and other dignitaries. The well-respected tycoon became one of Colorado's wealthiest men.

Barney Ford started adult education programs and was highly regarded as a black rights pioneer. He held up Colorado's bid for statehood until voting rights for black men was approved. In 1992, 145 years after his daring escape, Barney L. Ford was listed as one of the one hundred greatest Coloradoans. Eventually known as the "Black Baron of Colorado," he was posthumously inducted into the Colorado Business Hall of Fame.

THE ART OF PASSING
Ellen and William Craft:
Masters of Disguise

1848

Ellen nearly panicked when she saw Mr. Cray from Macon, Georgia—a gentleman she had served at Dr. Collins's supper table—coming down the aisle toward her. There were at least ten open seats on the train, yet he chose the one next to her. Ellen pulled her hat low and faced the window, hoping he would not see through her disguise. But Mr. Cray was intent on engaging his seatmate in a conversation.

Just the night before, Ellen Craft had been serving supper at Dr. and Mrs. Robert Collins's grand Georgia plantation. Ellen knew a great deal about the outside world from listening to the guests' conversations that occurred during such meals over the years. She and her husband planned on using the knowledge she gleaned to embark on a daring escape.

When Ellen was a child, given her light-skinned resemblance to her owner, Major James Smith, she had suffered terribly at the hands of a jealous Mrs. Smith. At age eleven she was given away to the Smiths' daughter as a wedding present. She had been with the Collins family ever since. Now the very color of her skin that had once caused her such misery just might allow Ellen and her husband William Craft to escape.

On December 21, 1848, she and William secured passes for the holidays from their respective owners. William worked for a cabinet-maker and Ellen was a house servant. Light-skinned Ellen was to don the disguise of an elderly and ailing gentleman planter. She would travel north with her dark-skinned "slave," her husband William, under the pretense of seeking medical attention in Philadelphia. The key to their success would rest in Ellen's ability to act the part of an infirm "Mr. Johnson." If caught, Ellen and William would most likely be separated and sold into hard labor.

Within the four days it took to formulate an escape plan, William collected the necessary components of Mr. Johnson's attire. His master allowed him to keep money he made working extra hours in a restaurant. William used some of his savings to purchase black boots, trousers, a white shirt, and a long black cloak.

Ellen's soft, beardless face needed to be covered up. It was decided that Mr. Johnson would be suffering from a severe toothache so that Ellen's face could be packed with a poultice and her head wrapped in bandages. An ascot scarf under her neck would hide her feminine lines. Just in case Ellen was asked to sign her name, her right arm would be put in a sling so as to render it useless, as she was illiterate. Atop her short cropped hair would be a stovepipe hat, and her eyes would be hidden behind a pair of green spectacles.

At last master and slave, Mr. Johnson and William, were ready to run for freedom. At the train station in Macon, Mr. Johnson purchased two tickets to Savannah, one in first class for "himself" and one in the Negro car for his servant. Immediately there was trouble.

After they were boarded, William saw his frantic employer out on the platform. Obviously his suspicions had been aroused, because he was searching the windows of the cars. Luckily the train pulled out of the station before he came to where William was seated.

It was the worst kind of luck when Mr. Cray, of all people, boarded the train. Since he had just been to Dr. Collins's house the previous evening, Ellen had spent several hours waiting on him. And now here he was sitting next to her. Ellen feigned deafness to avoid being engaged in a lengthy conversation. After a stressful exchange, Cray at last gave up and directed his conversation to another passenger. Fortunately, he was not going all two hundred miles from Macon to Savannah, Georgia. He departed the train a few stops later.

The Crafts boarded a steamer from Savannah, arriving in Charleston, South Carolina, without incident. Still disguised as Mr. Johnson, Ellen was readily welcomed at one of the finest hotels. But when she attempted to purchase two tickets aboard another steamer for Wilmington, North Carolina, she ran into a skeptical agent who insisted his registry must be signed. Using a deep voice, Ellen explained that as her right arm was broken, she could not possibly sign the ship's registry. Still, the man remained unmoved.

Just when the situation looked hopeless, a military officer from Charleston, whom Ellen had met on the first steamer, happened along and vouched that he indeed did know "Mr. Johnson."

After taking the steamer to Wilmington, Ellen and William took a train to Richmond, Virginia, and another to Fredericksburg, Virginia. At each stop they had to eavesdrop on other passengers to find out which train to board, since neither of them could read the signs. Next a steamer took them to Washington, DC, and from there trains took them to Baltimore, Maryland, and Philadelphia, Pennsylvania. These were anxious connections, during which both husband and wife constantly worried about being found out.

In addition to several close calls, there was always the fear that news of their escape would be forwarded along by telegraph to major cities and ports. Ellen avoided engaging with passengers and declined all offers from gentlemen of a cigar and drink, for she had no experience with either.

A captain, a slave trader, and a military officer each remonstrated Mr. Johnson for letting his uppity "nigger" dress too fine and for treating him too kindly. Ellen thanked the men for their advice and assured them that William would never run away. All offers to buy William were politely refused.

At one point, quick thinking allowed Ellen to hide her illiteracy. When a passenger offered his calling card, she put it in her pocket without looking at it, avoiding the possibility that she would appear to be reading it upside down.

Ellen and William Craft were almost discovered at their last stop. By law the railroad had to reimburse slave owners if runaways escaped on one of their trains. In Baltimore no one suspected Mr. Johnson of being female or black, but they questioned whether his slave might be a runaway. Consequently, he was asked to show proof of ownership.

Indignant, Mr. Johnson bellowed, "I bought tickets in Charleston to pass us through to Philadelphia, and you have no right to detain us here!" Just then the conductor from their last train passed by and verified that the slave had indeed accompanied Mr. Johnson from Washington. Still, the officer seemed unconvinced.

As their train was about to pull out of the station, the conductor shouted, "All aboard!" The officer began receiving disapproving stares from onlookers for the way he was detaining a sickly gentleman in front of the line—and for detaining them as well. At last he relented, saying, "Let this gentleman and slave pass." With a nod of thanks, William assisted the infirm Mr. Johnson hurriedly across the platform to their train to freedom.

Emotionally and physically spent, the fugitives rested fretfully. An exhausted William overslept and was temporarily separated from his "master" when they switched railcars. For the first time on the thousand-mile trip, William was not there to assist the infirm Mr. Johnson. Ellen grew panicked that William might have been apprehended. Later, upon finding each other, they privately shared a feeling of mutual relief and thanksgiving that their worst fears had not been realized, especially when they were so close to freedom.

On Christmas morning 1848, four long days after the start of their journey, Ellen and William Craft reached Philadelphia. The nighttime glow of lights sparkling in the distance meant freedom. On the train William had met a free black man who had told him of a boardinghouse run by abolitionists. Ellen and William acted on the tip and took a carriage ride to the house. It wasn't until they were alone in their room that Ellen gasped, "Thank God, William, we are safe!" and collapsed weeping into the arms of her husband. They fell on their knees that Christmas morning in prayerful gratitude for the best Christmas gift—a successful escape.

The landlord at the boardinghouse was confused to find Ellen Craft coming down to dinner with William. The exhausted travelers relayed their harrowing escape story to the astonished innkeeper. He notified members of the Pennsylvania Anti-slavery Society's Vigilance Committee, who were delighted to hear of the successful and ingenious escape.

The Vigilance Committee soon forwarded Ellen and William Craft to Boston, Massachusetts. They were legally married and set themselves up in the carpentry and seamstress business in Boston. Back home in Georgia, however, an irate Dr. and Mrs. Collins heard of the Crafts' much-publicized escape and were angered and embarrassed to have been outwitted. They sent slave catchers to Boston with warrants for their arrest, and the Crafts were nearly apprehended. The

Fugitive Slave Act of 1850, which allowed for the capture of fugitive slaves in free states, forced Ellen and William to take refuge overseas.

In December of 1850 the Crafts arrived in Liverpool, England, where they would live for nearly twenty years. They lectured and toured and received an education. Ellen was very proud that each of their five children was born free in England and never had to suffer under the yoke of slavery.

The Crafts' autobiography, *Running a Thousand Miles,* was published in 1860. The Civil War ended, and the Thirteenth Amendment to the US Constitution emancipated all slaves. In 1869 William and Ellen Craft and all but one of their children returned to the United States. Two years later, Ellen and William bought a plantation near Savannah, Georgia, not far from where they had formerly lived in bondage. They soon opened the Woodville Cooperative Farm School for black children on their land. In 1890 the Crafts moved to Charleston, South Carolina, where they lived into their seventies. They created a wealth of opportunities for the next generation during their nearly fifty years of freedom.

AT WHAT PRICE?
Captain Daniel Drayton
and the *Pearl*

1848

In April 1848 the citizens of Washington, DC, were celebrating a revolutionary wave moving across Europe. Democratic ideals seemingly appealed to the citizenry of France, Germany, Italy, and Austria. Americans gathered in Lafayette Park for bonfires, torch-lit processions, and passionate speeches proclaiming the right to life, liberty, and the pursuit of happiness.

On the fringes of this crowd stood a group of slaves and abolitionists who found the entire scene hypocritical. They wondered exactly how enslaved people in the nation's capital and elsewhere were free to pursue their life, liberty, and happiness. If abolitionist Captain Daniel Drayton could have spoken freely, he would have shouted to the crowd, "Nobody in this country will admit for a moment that there can be any such thing as property in a white man. The institution of slavery could not last for a day, if the slaves were all white." Instead Captain Drayton settled for knowing that the distractions of the night's celebration made the time ripe for a large-scale escape. Soon the revelers would be less some of their enslaved "citizens."

Two nights earlier, on April 13, 1848, the *Pearl* sailed into Washington, DC's Seventh Street wharf. Captain Daniel Drayton had charted the sailing vessel from Captain Sayres. Drayton would be in charge of smuggling the fugitive slaves aboard, while Sayres would man the fifty-four-ton bay-craft schooner.

When New York abolitionist William Chaplin hired Drayton, he'd implied that there would only be "a family or two" that needed safe passage. In reality this was to be the largest escape on the East Coast's Underground Railroad yet. Word of the strategic escape had spread to neighboring Georgetown and Alexandria.

The *Pearl* was docked under the Potomac River's high bank. As evening approached on Saturday, April 15, a light rain began to fall, but not enough to dampen the enthusiastic crowd celebrating in Lafayette Park. The fugitive slaves eased away from the crowd unnoticed. They crept past the few sparse buildings and open fields on the edge of Washington, DC, to arrive by the 11:00 p.m. deadline. The *Pearl*'s hull overflowed with fugitives. Captain Daniel Drayton counted more than seventy-six men, women, and children.

Before midnight the fastenings on the *Pearl* were cast off, and the group of hopefuls set sail under the cover of a thin blanket of fog. The path to freedom would take them 100 miles down the Potomac River, around Point Lookout, and 120 miles up the Chesapeake Bay, through the Delaware Canal to the Delaware River, and on to Frenchtown in New Jersey, a free state.

Soon after they set sail, the wind died down. Nervous tension could be felt among the passengers while they sat in the ominous calm. Captain Sayres dropped anchor so as not to be carried in the wrong direction by the tide coming in from the Atlantic. A sense of dread hung over everyone as they waited for the wind to increase. At daybreak a north breeze finally took them around Alexandria, Virginia. As the winds picked up, so did the spirits of the fugitive slaves huddled together in prayer and song in the ship's hold.

At dusk the *Pearl* reached Point Lookout on the mouth of the Potomac River. A fierce northerly wind prevented them from rounding the point. Captain Sayres, knowing the limits of his vessel, adamantly refused to take her out onto the open sea. Instead, he anchored the *Pearl* in Cornfield Harbor, Maryland, a safe refuge below the point. Again a sense of foreboding set in. The captains, crew, and passengers bedded down for the night around 9:00 p.m., having no choice but to wait it out.

While the *Pearl* was passing Alexandria, Virginia, residents of Alexandria, Washington, and Georgetown were awakening to discover their slaves missing. President James K. Polk, former first lady Dolley Madison, and thirty-nine other slave owners had slaves who had run off. The total value of their missing property was estimated at more than $100,000.

Meanwhile, unbeknownst to the passengers and crew of the *Pearl*, they had bigger troubles than the weather: They had been betrayed. A free black drayman named Judson Diggs had evidently transported two passengers to the *Pearl*, who apparently didn't have money to pay him. Additionally it was said that Diggs's advances toward one of the escapees had been rebuffed. Angered, Diggs turned them all in.

A posse of thirty-five men was rounded up and directed to the river. Less than twelve hours later, the posse had boarded the steamboat *Salem* and begun their pursuit.

At 2:00 a.m., with only 80 miles to go out of its 220-mile voyage, the *Pearl* was overtaken. The shocked passengers and crew were unarmed. The more violent men in the posse wished for an immediate lynching, but cooler heads prevailed. The steamer with the dejected prisoners headed back to the District of Columbia and anchored overnight at Fort Washington so as to arrive the following day. The slave catchers wanted to make an example of the shackled men, women, and children, parading them through the city in daylight.

Outraged slaveholders who thought their house servants and hotel and city workers were generally well treated determined to send them to the Deep South to be field hands. Most were sold to the slave-trading firm of Bruin & Hill out of Alexandria. After a stint in a slave pen, they would be sold down south to New Orleans.

The escape attempt of the *Pearl* made national headlines. The "Washington Riot" in the capital erupted when an angry mob insisted that an abolitionist newspaper press be destroyed in retaliation. Anti-slavery activists claimed the slave owners were hypocritical in light of the celebration of freedom that had occurred just two nights earlier.

Paul Jennings, a slave who had incited many to flee, had never boarded the ship, explaining that his sense of service and loyalty to a Washington senator kept him from going. He escaped prosecution, but feeling responsible for the fates of the fugitives he encouraged to escape, he consequently raised funds to purchase freedom for some of their family members. Most of the slaves, however, did not fare so well.

Captain Daniel Drayton was accused of being associated with the abolitionist William L. Chaplin, but he insisted he had worked alone. Drayton kept silent, as Chaplin allegedly had promised to take care of Drayton's wife and six children if he were ever arrested.

Captain Drayton and Captain Sayres stood trial for stealing property and assisting fugitives to escape. They were convicted of the latter on appeal and were remanded to prison until they could pay their heavy fines, which would have taken them a lifetime to raise. Four years later President Fillmore granted them an unconditional pardon. Captain Daniel Drayton never regretted his involvement.

CAUGHT BETWEEN
BLACK AND WHITE
Mary Walker and the Camerons

1848

As soon as the words escaped her mouth, Mary Walker wanted them back. The last thing she had envisioned for herself was being sent to the Deep South. However, she had voiced an unpopular opinion and, once crossed, Master Cameron always carried out his threats. If indeed Mary was sent away, she feared she would never see her children and mother again. Standing at a crossroad, Mary Walker needed to decide whether to run or not—before it was too late.

Judge Duncan Cameron of Raleigh, North Carolina, was one of the South's wealthiest slave owners, with plantations in three states served by nearly a thousand slaves. Four generations of Mary Walker's family had belonged to the Camerons. Since Mary was a trusted and favored house slave, Duncan Cameron never imagined she would leave his service. Mary thought otherwise.

In the summer of 1846, her seventy-year-old master took Mary Walker along with him to Philadelphia, Pennsylvania. He was summering there for six weeks with two of his adult daughters. By then Duncan Cameron was widowed and four of his six daughters had died from consumption (tuberculosis). Mary was attending Mildred Cameron, her master's twenty-four-year-old invalid daughter, who was seeking medical treatment in the city.

By 1848 the Camerons and Mary Walker had spent their third summer in Philadelphia, with little hope of a cure for Mildred's condition. Understandably, Duncan Cameron was ill-tempered, and perhaps Mary should have known better than to speak her mind with him.

Philadelphia was a hotbed of abolition activity. Over the past three summers, Mary had come in contact with free blacks who undoubtedly filled her head with notions of freedom. When Mary first came to Philadelphia in 1846, the law allowed slave owners to bring their slaves into the state for up to six months without altering their slave status. However, by 1848 a new law had allowed slaves to claim their freedom if their owners voluntarily brought them into the state. After three visits to Philadelphia, Mary had established a network of underground workers who were willing to help her escape bondage if she so chose.

When Mary spoke out of turn in July of 1848, Duncan Cameron was not about to tolerate such impudence. Perhaps Mary made mention of being away from her own family to care for his. Or perhaps she implied she could take her freedom if she wished due to the current law. Regardless, an irate Master Cameron threatened to send Mary to his son's plantation in Alabama—far from her own mother and children.

Mary Walker did not know how she could leave behind all she'd ever known. Her mind raced thinking about her grandmother, Aggy, and her mother, Silla, who had lived with the Camerons on their Stagville plantation in Durham, North Carolina. She thought about her years living with her mother on the Camerons' Fairntosh plantation, also in Durham. And now for the past twelve years she had resided with the Camerons at their mansion in Raleigh, where Master Cameron was president of the Bank of North Carolina. Her mother and children lived with Mary.

Mary panicked at the thought of being separated from her children. Her eldest son, Frank, was sixteen. Her daughter, Agnes, was eleven, and her youngest son, Bryant, was four years old. Mary had heard that Paul Cameron, Duncan's son, was looking to buy another plantation in Louisiana or Mississippi—and he was known to whip slaves. Paul Cameron was making preparations to take slaves, animals, and materials with him. Being sent to the Deep South meant Mary would have virtually no chance of being reunited with her children. She had little time to decide.

Mary Walker's choice that hot summer day in July 1848 came down to being sent into exile or starting a new life—alone. If she stayed with the Camerons, she would be sent away. If she escaped while the Camerons were still summering in Philadelphia, she could attempt to free her children one day. The choice was an agonizing one, but Mary made it. The Camerons were shocked when Mary left.

Duncan Cameron and his two daughters returned to Raleigh, North Carolina, on August 9, 1848, without their trusted and favored slave. Mary Walker disappeared on the streets of Philadelphia the day prior to their departure.

Mary tried to comfort herself with the knowledge that the Camerons usually treated their slaves with kindness, especially the Walker family. The Camerons spoke fondly of their "black and white family." Their children played together—until obedience called and it came time for the black children to serve the white children. However, the Camerons kept the slave families together and they were well cared for. Still, it broke Mary's heart to not say good-bye to her family. Like her grandmother and mother before her, Mary had her first child at age fourteen—and also like them, had children fathered by white men. This she did not want for her own daughter, Agnes. Mary was determined to create a better life for her family.

Mary Walker, her mother, and her children were all mulattoes, of mixed white and black heritage. Mary was a fair-skinned thirty-year-old woman who could nearly pass for white. She was of slight build with dark straight hair and light eyes with a tint of blue. She had been taught to read and write, having been tutored along with the Camerons' daughters. She was also a skilled seamstress like her mother. Hopefully these advantages would help her make a living in Philadelphia.

The network of agents involved in the underground work of assisting fugitive slaves helped Mary Walker begin her new life. She came to reside in the household of James Lesley Jr. and worked as a seamstress, saving every dollar to help secure her family's freedom.

Pennsylvania's Personal Liberty Law protected Mary for two years. However, it was superseded by the Fugitive Slave Law of 1850, which allowed owners to pursue fugitive slaves out of state. Now anyone caught aiding or concealing a runaway slave could be imprisoned for twelve months and receive a $1,000 fine. Mary was no longer safe—especially since the Camerons had returned to Philadelphia for additional medical treatment for Mildred, and at times lodged less than two blocks from their former slave.

In November 1850 James Lesley sent Mary Walker farther north to live with his cousin in Milton, outside Boston, Massachusetts. Peter and Susan Lesley gave Mary sanctuary and adopted her quest to secure her children's freedom as their own personal undertaking. They would provide employment, protection, and emotional support in the coming years. Mary continued working as a seamstress and confided the details of her life to them.

When Peter Lesley's work took them back to Philadelphia, Mary stayed on in Cambridge, Massachusetts, to care for Mrs. Lesley's mother, Anne Jean Lyman (great-grandmother of Franklin Delano Roosevelt). Mary was a devoted caregiver and companion in the years to come, despite suffering from headaches, rheumatism, and depression that stemmed from the traumatic decision to leave her children behind.

After five years, however, it was time to reclaim her family. Mary had saved enough money to buy one child, her daughter Agnes. When Master Cameron died in 1853, the fate of her children became uncertain. She had to act quickly before they might be sold.

Word reached Mary that her eldest son, Frank, age twenty, had escaped around 1852, four years after Mary left. The Camerons set out to capture him, but with his light skin, green eyes, and freckles, he could easily blend in with white society. Mary was uncertain how the Camerons would feel about selling Agnes since Frank's escape.

Peter and Susan Lesley helped Mary find an intermediary to arrange the offer of money for Agnes. A Reverend Thomas Moore enlisted the help of a clergyman in Raleigh to inquire about the sale, but nothing came to fruition. Next Mary enlisted a close friend of Mildred Cameron's to inquire on her behalf. Nothing came of those negotiation efforts either.

Mary then decided to plan an escape for her family. In July of 1854 the Lesleys contacted the leader of Boston's Underground Railroad, who paid an agent, James Price, $300 for a covert rescue operation to secure seventeen-year-old Agnes and ten-year-old Bryant. After two attempts no success came from the four-hundred-mile trips from Philadelphia to Raleigh, North Carolina. It was never determined if the agent met impossible odds on his rescue missions or if he was a swindler who took their money with little effort on his end.

Next Mary hired an agent on her own to retrieve her children and another to search for her son who had escaped. Neither effort was successful. Abolitionists Frederick Douglass, Henry Ward Beecher, and Harriet Beecher Stowe, author of *Uncle Tom's Cabin*, were contacted, but nothing came of it.

In September 1859 Peter Lesley made a dramatic appeal by writing an emotional letter to the invalid Mildred Cameron in Raleigh. He conveyed how Mary's eleven-year separation from her children had caused her extreme heartbreak, anxiety, and grief. There was no reply from Mildred.

The start of the Civil War put an end to any communications attempted by the Cameron servants to provide Mary with information about her children. Yet Mary continued her efforts, asking Union soldiers near Raleigh if there was any word on her children's welfare. In 1864 Mary accepted an invitation to aid emancipated slaves on South Carolina's Sea Islands, where she learned that freedom did not necessarily ensure a secure future.

Mary Walker had tried six times to liberate her family, from offering to buy them outright to attempting a rescue and making an emotional appeal for their release. All of Mary's relentless pursuits failed despite numerous clandestine meetings with leaders on the Underground Railroad, coded letters, and meetings with secret agents.

It was the end of the Civil War that finally reunited the Walker family. Union General Oliver O. Howard, who oversaw Raleigh's occupation, was familiar with Mary's search for her children. The general found Agnes and Bryant, now twenty-eight and twenty-one years respectively, at Duncan Cameron's mansion in Raleigh. Her mother, Silla, had died. Mary's children learned their mother was in Cambridge, Massachusetts, and had been working for their release ever since she left.

After seventeen long years of separation, Mary's captive heart was freed. Bryant arrived in Cambridge on June 28, 1865, and Agnes and her husband arrived on July 14. Mary Walker was forty-seven. As for her son Frank, he was rumored to be in New Jersey, but mother and son were never reunited.

Mary's broad circle of friends helped the Walkers find employment in Cambridge. Together they fought their battles and demons to survive in a land foreign to them as free people.

In 1870 the Howes, Mary Walker's former employers, bought a house in an upscale neighborhood on Brattle Street and turned the deed over to Mary. With its spreading chestnut tree, Number 54 Brattle Street, three blocks from poet Henry Wadsworth Longfellow's mansion, was large enough for Mary's children and grandchildren. In 1840 Longfellow had made the Cambridge residence famous by immortalizing the home, which had belonged to the village smithy, in his poem "The Village Blacksmith."

Mary Walker died on November 10, 1872, at age fifty-four after enjoying seven years reunited with her children. Mary had understood what the struggle for economic freedom would entail for mixed-race children caught between black and white, and had the foresight to secure lodging for her family's future. The rent-free house was willed to her grandchildren and stayed in the family until 1912. Today it is a Cambridge landmark in Harvard Square.

The lives of Mary Walker and Peter and Susan Lesley, who sympathized with Mary, were forever entwined. Their joint mission to free her family grew into deep affection for one another. In 2008 a descendant of Mary Walker met with a descendant of Susan Lesley—bridging a new friendship that had once connected their forbearers long before them.

THE ELEVENTH HOUR
Samuel D. Burris, Abolitionist

1848

Samuel D. Burris was stripped of his clothes and dragged nearly naked to the slave auction block in Dover, Delaware. Poked and prodded by potential buyers, the slave owners felt his muscles, checked his head for lice, looked at his back to see if he had been whipped, and probed in his mouth to inspect his teeth. His worst nightmares were coming true.

Samuel D. Burris was a free, educated black man. He had been born in Willow Grove, Delaware, in 1808. A black person in the state of Delaware was considered free unless proven otherwise, but ads offering rewards for runaway slaves appeared frequently in newspapers, and sometimes free black people were abducted because they resembled descriptions of runaways. They were kidnapped and taken back to slave states without the benefit of a trial.

The free state of Delaware bordered Maryland (a slave state) on the west and Pennsylvania (a free state) on the north. As an adult Burris had moved with his family to Philadelphia, where there was a vibrant community of abolitionists. He partnered with Thomas Garrett of Wilmington, Delaware, and John Hunn, a Maryland Quaker, in working on a system of secreting fugitive slaves to Canada.

In time Burris came to be recognized as an agent of the Underground Railroad. He would often go deep into Maryland to conduct a group of fugitives northward, stopping at various stations along the Underground Railroad. Burris's belief in what he did and his success as both an agent and conductor may have allowed him to think he was invincible.

Proponents of slavery were suspicious of Samuel Burris, and no doubt kept a watchful eye on him. In 1848 he was apprehended in Dover, Delaware, while transporting a band of runaway slaves and was thrown in jail. When news of his capture reached John Hunn and Thomas Garrett, they contacted the Anti-slavery Society in Philadelphia. Though the members of the society had not always sanctioned Burris's actions, they were well aware of his services in bringing slaves to freedom. They set out to do what they could for him.

Burris sat in prison for months while he awaited trial. Meanwhile, preparation for a legal battle was moving forward just one hundred yards away in the state capitol. James M. McKim of the Anti-slavery Executive Committee took particular interest in Burris's case. McKim and his office, along with John Hunn and Thomas Garrett, implored the governor to intervene on Burris's behalf. The governor turned a deaf ear.

At Burris's trial it was determined that legislation enacted in 1837 should be upheld. The law clearly stated that any free black person convicted of assisting fugitive slaves would be sold into slavery himself for a period of time determined by the court. The judge gave Burris a sentence of seven years of servitude. A shocked and dejected Burris was led out of the courtroom. There would be no appeal.

In September of 1848 Burris was led down the steps of the Delaware State House to Dover's town center. He was made to stand with the very people he had risked his life to save. Dejected and demoralized, no doubt stunned by man's inhumanity to man, he was pushed roughly to the forefront. The auctioneer began to enumerate his fine physical attributes. Burris caught the eye of his friend John Hunn among the group of spectators, and Hunn's sympathetic countenance said it all. There was absolutely nothing he could do.

Two slave traders from Baltimore were bidding against each other for Samuel Burris. Another trader, a Southern gentleman new to the area, seemed to have a particular interest in him. The man postured as if he had a great deal of money to spend. One of the Baltimore dealers was in the lead, with a bid of $500. The Southern buyer upped the ante to $600, giving the impression that he would be increasing the bid by increments of $100. The dealers from Baltimore hesitated. The slight pause gave the Southern buyer the advantage. The auctioneer cried "Sold!" and pounded his gavel. The sound reverberated in Burris's ears.

John Hunn watched dejectedly as Burris was led off the block. Those who had come to witness Burris's punishment for breaking the law had smug looks on their faces. Hunn only shook his head and sadly walked away.

But the Southern buyer who had purchased Burris seemed indifferent. He picked up his bill of sale and led his new slave property away. When they were out of sight of the slaveholders, his "owner" whispered into Burris's ear, "You have been bought with abolition gold." It must have been hard for Burris to believe. It had all been a ruse.

The "Southern slave owner" who bought him was none other than Isaac S. Flint, an avid abolitionist from Wilmington, Delaware. James McKim from Philadelphia's Anti-slavery Society did not dare let John Hunn or Thomas Garrett pose as the slave trader, for fear of being recognized. Instead someone with a low profile was chosen. McKim had raised the necessary funds to buy Burris right out from under the nose of the slave traders. Under an assumed name, Flint had been studying the Baltimore slave traders until he could mimic them perfectly. Fortunately the bidding had stopped when it did; if the amount had been too high, Burris's fate would have been sealed.

In a strange reversal of roles, Samuel D. Burris was now a passenger on the same Underground Railroad he had previously supported. He was conducted to Philadelphia and reunited with his family.

That same year, John Hunn and Thomas Garrett were tried and fined for assisting other fugitives. It nearly bankrupted the men, but they continued their work for freedom's cause.

After a few years in Philadelphia, Burris took his family to California in 1852. He kept abreast of the Underground Railroad's activities back East, however, and did what he could to help. He also assisted former slaves who had come to California looking for a better life. After the Civil War, when there was a particular need to assist the freed slaves seeking refuge in Washington, DC, Burris contacted the black churches in San Francisco to raise funds for the cause. In 1869 he died at the age of sixty-one, eulogized as a man who had devoted his entire life to the fighting of injustice.

THE LETTER OF THE LAW
The Case of *Daggs v. Frazier, et al.*

1848

Sam Slaughter, a slave catcher hired by Ruel Daggs, had been fol-lowing muddy wagon-wheel ruts for hours, convinced he was on the heels of the fugitives. When he spotted a covered wagon stopped beside a creek, he thought the chase was over. Slaughter was sorely disappointed, however, to only discover three white men returning from a fishing trip near Des Moines, Iowa.

Jonathan Frazier, who was the driver of the wagon, and his two companions agreed to ride on together with Slaughter toward the nearby town of Salem—so as not to arouse his suspicion. Meanwhile, the fugitive slaves hidden off the road all held their breath. Jonathan Frazier, son of the leader of Iowa's Anti-slavery Friends, was actually transporting Ruel Daggs's runaways. He had wisely sensed they were being followed and hurried all nine slaves into the bushes.

Two evenings earlier, on June 1, 1848, twenty-two-year-old John Walker snuck back onto Ruel Daggs's farm. He had escaped several months earlier but had returned for his wife, Mary, and their baby.

Six other slaves had decided to run away with Walker that night: Sam Fulcher; his wife, Dorcas; their eighteen-year-old daughter, Julia; ten-year-old daughter, Martha; a younger son named William; and their youngest son, who was three. The fugitives had no idea that they were soon to become embroiled in a prolonged federal court case—the first of its kind dealing with the Underground Railroad in Iowa.

The band of hopeful fugitives had headed first to the home of Richard Leggen after escaping from Ruel Daggs's farm. From there the slaves managed a hazardous Des Moines River crossing on a crude raft, just below Farmington in southeastern Iowa. The deluge of rain continued all day Saturday, while the men, women, and children took cover under trees along the shore, awaiting transportation. They had gotten all the way to Salem, Iowa, twenty-five miles north of the Missouri–Iowa border, before almost being apprehended by Sam Slaughter.

Ruel Daggs's farm was nestled in the gently rolling hills of northeastern Missouri. It was less than thirty miles from the free state of Iowa, which may have been why Daggs was now missing nine of his sixteen slaves. Daggs had a reputation as an honest, fair man who treated his slaves well, but he supposed that they might have gotten wind of the fact that he was thinking of selling them south. Daggs had come to the realization that living in a border state enticed slaves to run off and had therefore decided to sell them before he lost valuable property.

Seventy-three-year-old Ruel Daggs put his son, William, and a neighbor, James McClure, in charge of regaining his slave property. They had hired Sam Slaughter in Salem, Iowa, to assist in their search.

On Sunday morning Slaughter and McClure widened their search, eventually finding Daggs's nine slaves hidden about two hundred yards off another road along Little Red Cedar Creek. They had been on the run for three days.

The leader, John Walker, resisted recapture but was finally restrained. Since it was such a large group of runaways, the slave catchers decided they needed assistance. Slaughter took off to secure additional hired hands to manage their return to Missouri while McClure guarded the captives.

By the time Slaughter returned, twelve abolitionists had surrounded McClure and the slaves. One of them said he would "wade in Missouri blood" before the men, women, and children were hauled away. No one was going anywhere without seeing an officer of the law first.

The motley group of adversaries all walked to Salem to see the justice of the peace, Nelson Gibbs. An unruly crowd of onlookers gathered. The confusion made it difficult for Slaughter to keep track of the slaves. John Walker slipped away in the crowd, and Slaughter soon feared that he would lose the rest of them.

Justice Gibbs presided over the divisive crowd of nearly one hundred pro-slavery and abolitionist townsfolk who had gathered. Both groups were loudly voicing their opinions as to how the situation should be handled.

Attorneys were appointed for the slaves. In just a few hours, Justice Gibbs ruled against the slave catchers. Not only did Slaughter and McClure not have arrest warrants, they also couldn't personally identify the slaves.

Slaughter and McClure were acting as agents for Daggs by verbal agreement only. They had no written documentation proving they were acting on his behalf. Justice Gibbs, who was an antislavery magistrate, conducted an informal inquiry and decided his court did not hold jurisdiction. He declared that the fugitives were free to go. Sam Fulcher mounted a horse that was offered him. A man in the crowd handed him his three-year-old son and they rode away. The rest of the slaves were assisted on their way to freedom by antislavery townsfolk. McClure and Slaughter vowed revenge for being robbed of their captives.

A few days later the two slave catchers, along with over one hundred armed Missourians, returned to Iowa and descended upon Salem, which had a population of just five hundred people. They set up roadblocks going out of town and began searching for Ruel Daggs's slaves.

Unsuccessful in their search, McClure and Slaughter enlisted the help of a local pro-slavery man who identified all those who had been involved in assisting the slaves to escape. The Missourians arrested over ten men using blank warrants issued by a constable in another town. Some of the men included Jonathan Frazier and John H. Pickering. Frazier had driven the Walker and Fulcher slave families in the wagon and barely evaded Slaughter the first time. Pickering's horses had pulled the wagon. All were held captive in a hotel by the Missourians. A Henry County sheriff arranged for their release after they signed a recognizance to appear at a hearing in federal district court.

The angry Missourians threatened to burn the Iowa town and start lynching abolitionists if they did not find the fugitives. Antislavery supporters from a town twenty miles southeast of Salem came to answer the Missouri mob's threats and assure peace.

Four of the nine slaves were eventually recaptured by the Missourians and returned to Ruel Daggs: Sam Fulcher's wife, Dorcas; their daughters, Julia and Martha; and their son William. Sam Fulcher and his three-year-old son, who had ridden away on a horse the day of the first trial, escaped. John Walker, who had instigated the escape from Daggs's farm, made it to freedom in Canada with his wife and baby.

Ruel Daggs sought compensation for the loss of service of his nine slaves, and brought suit against nineteen men in a US district court in Iowa in September of 1848. The case of *Daggs v. Frazier, et al.* dragged on for two years.

According to the Fugitive Slave Act of 1793, the US Constitution recognized the institution of slavery and upheld the right of the slave owner to reclaim his property from another state. Iowans disallowed slavery. The jury took two hours to find six of the defendants in violation of the Constitution, maintaining that the men had no right to release another man's property and that no moral law was to stand above the Constitution. Judge John J. Dyer overruled the jury and found just five of the defendants guilty on two counts of harboring and concealing those they knew to be slaves.

The men were fined $2,900, presumably the combined market value and loss of services assigned to the five fugitive slaves who had escaped. There is no record that Ruel Daggs ever received any of the money after the prolonged court battle, and it's unlikely he ever did: All but one of the men charged had previously transferred their assets to trusted individuals.

THIS SIDE UP
Henry Brown's Mail Delivery

1849

At the age of thirty-four, and upside down in a fetal position, Henry Brown was ready to be born into a new life. It was a tight fit, folding his five-foot-eight, two-hundred-pound frame into a claustrophobic wooden crate. The blood pressure in his head and the sweltering heat was almost unbearable. His muscles were cramping, and the lack of fresh air in his dark enclosure was making him light-headed. And yet, it would all be worth it if only he could be released into freedom.

Henry Brown had been born the first time around 1815 on a slave plantation in Louisa County, Virginia. In 1830 when his master died, he had seen his family split apart, divvied up among his master's heirs. Henry was hired out to work in a tobacco-manufacturing plant in Richmond, Virginia, at age fourteen. He was allowed to keep a portion of his earnings, enabling him to later provide a modest house for his wife, Nancy, and their three children. Though he was given preferential treatment, it never made up for the pain of having been separated from his family during his childhood. Eighteen years later, he was to suffer the pain of separation yet again.

Henry returned home from the tobacco factory for lunch one day to find his wife and children missing. He was stunned to learn they had been put on the auction block, sold, and imprisoned until their departure the next day. His wife's owner, Mr. Cotrell, had previously promised not to sell Henry's wife or their children if Henry paid him $50 a year. Cotrell collected the money and broke his promise. When Henry begged to buy his own family, he was told, "You can get another wife."

A bewildered Brown watched in abject horror as 350 dejected souls filed by, heading toward their new home in North Carolina. Five wagonloads of anguished children wailed for their parents. Henry's eldest child called for him with outstretched arms. His wife of twelve years was led along in a chain gang like an animal, stupefied with a rope around her neck. Henry stood engulfed in grief— stripped of his manhood, deprived of the ability to rescue, provide, and care for his family.

Henry Brown was incensed at the injustice of losing his family. He vowed to run away and retrieve them, but first he had to let time pass so as not to bring undue attention upon himself. Five months later, with little left to lose, Henry decided to make a break for freedom. A bold plan came to him: "The idea suddenly flashed across my mind of shutting myself up in a box, and getting myself conveyed as dry goods to a free state." He only needed to survive the journey.

Henry consulted with Samuel A. Smith, a white shoe dealer in Richmond, whom he could trust to help execute the plan. Smith traveled to Philadelphia, Pennsylvania, on Henry's behalf to make the necessary arrangements with the Vigilance Committee, a branch of the Pennsylvania Anti-slavery Society established to assist runaway slaves. They were informed to look for a box containing human cargo.

John Mattaner, a black carpenter, was asked to construct a hickory box large enough to hold a person but small enough so as not to arouse suspicion of its contents. Henry had previously visited the train depot to ascertain the various-sized boxes coming through. A free black dentist, James C. A. Smith, outfitted the crate with baize—a coarse, feltlike, napped fabric—to afford some comfort inside the small compartment. Henry would contort his body into a ball, knees tight against his chest in a cushion of cloth meant to keep him from shifting about inside the wooden crate.

Having made all the necessary arrangements, Henry Brown just needed a pass from his master that would allow him to be away from the tobacco factory. He intentionally doused his finger with some corrosive acid, oil of vitriol, that he had acquired to secure a brief reprieve from work. Injured and temporarily freed from his responsibilities, he set his plan into action.

On March 29, 1849, Henry gulped a last breath of fresh air and let himself be confined inside his box with nothing more than a few biscuits, a beef bladder of water, a hat to fan himself, and a gimlet (a screwlike tool used to bore air holes). The box was secured with hickory hoops by Samuel A. Smith, who crated Henry Brown inside.

There were substantial risks of being arrested and prosecuted for everyone involved in Henry's audacious escape plan. A large box delivered to the Anti-slavery Society might cause suspicion. Therefore the crate was addressed to "William H. Johnson, 131 Arch Street, Philadelphia, Pennsylvania." The words "This Side Up With Care" were neatly printed atop the container. That afternoon Smith sent a telegram to the Pennsylvania Anti-slavery Society office in Philadelphia stating, "Your case of goods is shipped and will arrive tomorrow morning."

Henry's 350-mile journey from Richmond, Virginia, to Philadelphia, Pennsylvania, began at 4:00 a.m. The box was put on an open horse cart and taken to the express office. The first leg of the trip was made upside down, with no regard for the printed directions. The box was then placed on its side on the baggage car en route to the steamer ship, then loaded upside down again on the steamer itself, where it remained for a period of ninety minutes. Henry's head pulsated with excruciating pain, and his eyeballs bulged from the pressure of the blood rushing to his head. Yet, for Henry Brown, risking death was favorable over being enslaved.

Voices on deck the steamship indicated that people were coming and going. Henry couldn't try to roll the box himself for fear of being discovered. But then as if in answer to his prayers, he heard two men complaining about how they'd been standing for such a length of time. They toppled his box over on its side to make a seat. The unbearable pressure on Henry's head and neck was relieved just in time.

There was more rough handling during the remaining overland journey, during which he was placed right side up, then dropped. He was nearly left behind at the station due to lack of space aboard the luggage train, but at the last minute the box was loaded—upside down. Eventually he was placed right side up, and remained that way until his arrival at the Adams Express Office in Philadelphia.

Henry Brown arrived at the depot at 3:00 a.m. He was picked up at 6:00 a.m. Again, to avoid suspicion, E. M. Davis, an abolitionist who dealt with the Adams Express Office, sent a hired man to retrieve the box and bring it to the Pennsylvania Anti-slavery Society office, where members of the Vigilance Committee awaited his arrival.

On the morning of March 30, several members of the committee gathered inside the office with curtains drawn: J. M. McKim, Professor Cleveland, Lewis Thompson, and William Still—all dedicated abolitionists. The doors were secured, and the gentlemen looked uneasily at each other, dreading Henry Brown might not have survived the ordeal. They rapped upon the box. "Is all right within?" With the reply, "All right!" the elated men broke open the box and gingerly lifted the cramped Henry Brown to his feet.

Henry felt faint, perhaps from the sudden release of his confinement, the rush of fresh air, or simply the emotion of the moment. He had survived nearly twenty-seven hours entombed inside the suffocating compartment. After the newly freed man, soaked with perspiration, was revived, he quoted a hymn of thanksgiving: "I waited patiently for the Lord . . . and he heard my calling."

News of Henry's bold, imaginative escape was well received, and he soon found a new life on the antislavery lecture circuit. He was dubbed Henry "Box" Brown, and his amazing tale of escape drew empathy and support for the antislavery sentiment. He took letters of introduction with him to Boston and New York, sitting on a passenger seat of the train this time—not crated in a box. Telegrams from the abolitionists in Philadelphia recommending him were sent ahead.

Seven months later Samuel A. Smith, the shoe dealer in Richmond, was sentenced to eight years in prison for assisting with two similar escape plans. He spent five of those months in solitary confinement, chained in a four-by-eight-foot cell. James C. A. Smith, the free black man who had outfitted the crate, was also convicted, but paid $900 for an attorney who was able to acquit him.

After a year on the lecture circuit, Henry Brown came close to being captured in Providence, Rhode Island, and returned to slavery— which would have been sanctioned by the Fugitive Slave Law of 1850. Abolitionists wisely secreted him to England with the aid of workers on the Underground Railroad. For a while Henry "Box" Brown and James C. A. Smith toured together on antislavery speaking engagements. They took along a several-thousand-foot painted canvas titled *The Mirror of Slavery* as a pictorial representation of slavery's evils.

Henry Brown was criticized in the press by antislavery supporters for publicizing his mode of escape. Since similar attempts were foiled, it prohibited others from using the same method. Brown, however, insisted that through his notoriety, by educating the public on the horrors of slavery and inciting them to take action, he could do more for the antislavery movement than by remaining silent.

Sadly, Henry Brown was never reunited with his family. But his life narrative, published both in the United States and in England, did much to bolster support for the abolitionist movement.

READ ALL ABOUT IT!
Lear Green's Love Story

1850

With each step he took down the crowded city streets, James Noble's anger increased. He was a man on a mission. His destination on that October day in 1850 was the newspaper office of the *Baltimore Sun*, where he intended to place an ad. When the residents of Baltimore, Maryland, picked up their newspapers, they would soon read:

$150 REWARD.
Ran away from the subscriber, on Sunday night, 27th inst., my NEGRO GIRL, Lear Green, about 18 years of age, black complexion, round-featured, good-looking and ordinary size; she had on and with her when she left, a tan-colored silk bonnet, a dark plaid silk dress, a light mouslin delaine, also one watered silk cape and one tan colored cape. I have reason to be confident that she was persuaded off by a negro man named Wm. Adams, black, quick spoken, 5 feet 10

inches high, a large scar on one side of his face, running down in a ridge by the corner of his mouth, about 4 inches long, barber by trade, but works mostly about taverns, opening oysters, &c. He has been missing about a week; he had been heard to say he was going to marry the above girl and ship to New York, where it is said his mother resides. The above reward will be paid if said girl is taken out of the State of Maryland and delivered to me; or fifty dollars if taken in the State of Maryland.

JAMES NOBLE,
No. 153 Broadway, Baltimore.

James Noble had inherited his slave girl, Lear Green, from his mother-in-law when she was quite young. Noble and his wife had practically raised her—a well-dressed young woman of polish and grace—and this was how their house servant repaid them? It was preposterous! Noble was a respected merchant in town, and he did not appreciate that his slave girl had just up and slipped away.

The Nobles had kept Lear Green as busy as possible, but Lear had apparently still found time to acquaint herself with the free man William Adams. James Noble later berated himself for not realizing that Adams was sweet on his Lear.

William Adams and Lear Green had indeed fallen in love. In fact, William had repeatedly proposed to Lear. But Lear had told him the same thing she had told her own mother: that she would never marry. Any children born to her while she was a slave would become slaves themselves, and she wouldn't be able to abide that. Lear wanted her children to be born free.

William therefore had incentive to seek Lear's freedom. Together they came up with an outlandish and dangerous plan—one that could only succeed with the cooperation of William's mother, a free woman who lived in New York.

Mrs. Adams accepted her son's invitation to visit him and traveled to Baltimore. There she learned about the escape plan to secret Lear Green out of town. Both William and Mrs. Adams had to be willing to risk their own free status to assist Lear. His mother agreed.

Mrs. Adams prepared for her journey back to New York aboard the Ericsson Line of steamers. An old sailor's chest with leather straps was arranged with items for the trip home. Inside she put a pillow, a quilt, some clothes, water, food—and her future daughter-in-law, Lear Green. William fastened ropes around the chest and carefully lifted the trunk with its precious cargo onto a wagon. When they arrived at the wharf, Mrs. Adams presented her ticket and walked aboard the steamer.

By 1850 the passenger lists for all vessels were being inspected for fugitive slaves. Any ship caught smuggling slaves had to pay $500, to both the state and to the slave owner. Fortunately, no one opened the chest to inspect it before loading it onto the steamship.

Though Mrs. Adams was a free woman, discriminatory practices prohibited her from being seated with the white passengers. Blacks were relegated to the open deck of the ship in the luggage and cargo area, which was exactly where Mrs. Adam's sailor's chest had been placed.

The steamer pulled away from its dock in Baltimore. Packed tight inside the trunk, Lear Green could feel the rocking of the ship but could not partake in the beautiful Chesapeake Bay scenery. The ship headed northeast through the Chesapeake and Delaware Canal, then up the Delaware River. Lear had begun her suffocating eighteen hours of confinement. If she were discovered, it would put not only her own life and safety in peril, but also those of her loved ones.

Mrs. Adams looked around on deck. When no one was nearby, she loosened the ropes and secretly lifted the lid a few times during the night. This allowed her to check on Lear's welfare and provide her with some fresh air.

The ship docked in Philadelphia without any of the handlers questioning the contents of the trunk. Still confined, Lear and the sailor's chest were delivered to friends of Mrs. Adams on Barley Street. From there it was forwarded by means of another jolting carriage ride to the office of the Anti-slavery Society in Philadelphia. William Still, chairman of the Vigilance Committee, opened the trunk, thankful to find Lear Green alive.

Lear remained at the Still residence for several days before being moved to her final destination, Elmira, New York. William Adams had successfully made his way from Baltimore without being caught and was anxiously waiting for Lear.

The young couple was soon married and lived in Elmira, where William's mother resided. They enjoyed three years together. Sadly, Lear died of unknown causes at age twenty-one. If it was any consolation to her grieving husband, her last years were spent in freedom.

William Still so admired Lear Green for her courage and determination to seek freedom at all costs that he had a photo taken of her exiting the trunk and was said to have kept the sailor's chest as a reminder of her valiant efforts. He later said of her that she had "won for herself a strong claim to a high place among the heroic women of the nineteenth century."

REMEMBER ME
William Still's Discovery

1850

When the door to William Still's office on North Fifth Street opened on August 1, 1850, it revealed a tall, middle-aged man named Peter Friedman. He had traveled hundreds of miles from Alabama to find his family and had been directed by local churches to the office of the Pennsylvania Anti-slavery Society. He was hoping they might be able to help him. But even in his wildest imaginings, he couldn't have been prepared for what he learned that day.

Twenty-nine-year-old William Still wasn't yet known as the "Father of the Underground Railroad," but during his lifetime the energetic young black man would work his way up from being clerk, field organizer, and secretary to chairman of the Acting Committee of the Pennsylvania Anti-slavery Society. Currently, as secretary, his job was to personally interview fugitives who had made their way to Philadelphia, determine what assistance they needed, and keep a record of all expenditures. His records would later help fugitive slaves locate long-separated family members.

William listened attentively and took notes as Peter Friedman, nearly twenty years his senior, unfolded the saga of his life. As a free black man, it was hard for William Still to imagine undergoing such trials and tribulations as being sold like a piece of property and being beaten unmercifully. He seemed to have little in common with the man on the other side of his desk—or so he thought.

Peter, now fifty years old, had been separated from his mother for more than forty years. His early memories were admittedly dim when trying to recall exactly where they had lived or what his mother and sisters had looked like. Too much time had passed. The two men studied each other with regret. With so little to go on, it was doubtful there would be a happy ending to Peter's search.

Peter recounted the main events in his life. He had lived the better part of it in Kentucky and Alabama, a slave under various masters. He was the second eldest of four children, and while his father had been able to buy his own freedom, Peter, his mother, and his siblings had remained slaves. He remembered one failed escape attempt when he was six years old, and vaguely recalled a kidnapping after which he and his brother never saw their mother and sisters again. Peter had suffered a terrible loss later in life when his brother died at the hands of a cruel master at age thirty-three.

It wasn't until Peter Friedman was an adult that he had been able to buy his freedom. Now he was seeking assistance for purchasing his wife and children, whom he had left behind in Alabama. Regrettably, Peter did not know his real last name; Friedman was the name of his last owner. He also could not say exactly where he had been born.

William Still mentally noted how his own life contrasted so sharply with that of the man sitting across from him. For one thing, William had been born in New Jersey and was raised free. He was the youngest of eighteen children. His deceased father, Levin, had purchased his own freedom when he was a young adult, but his mother,

Charity, had been a runaway. She had escaped slavery with their two daughters, who were William's oldest sisters, forty-four years ago. Her two sons, William's oldest brothers he'd never met before, had been left behind in slavery. Charity had been reunited with William's father and had changed her name for safety's sake.

William Still needed more information, and asked Peter to recall any details that might provide some clues. Peter remembered that he had been five years old when his father had gone north. A year later, his mother had taken all four of her children with her on her first escape attempt. Peter was then six years old, his brother Levin was eight, and their sisters were younger. Their arduous journey to freedom was short-lived. It was somewhere along the Delaware River, perhaps near Philadelphia, that slave catchers had come in the middle of the night and abducted them all, dragging them back to their owner.

Peter's mother was locked up for three months to ensure that she would not run away again, but that did not deter her. A few weeks after her release, Peter and Levin had awoken to find their mother and sisters gone. Out of spite, their enraged owner, Saunders Griffin, sold the confused and distraught boys to Kentucky so that their mother would never find them. Before they were taken away, the boys' grandmother told them never to forget the names of their parents, Levin and Sidney, and to remember that they were up north of the Delaware River.

William Still put down his pen and furrowed his brow as he listened further. Peter told about how he and his brother had been sold and resold, working in brickyards, tobacco factories, and cotton fields, sometimes enduring whippings at the hands of overseers and masters. As Peter talked about searching for his wife, Vina, and his children—Levin, Peter, and Catharine—a terrible sadness came over him. William had seen that same look on the face of his own mother, who often prayed for the two sons she had left behind.

It seemed that William Still did have some things in common with Peter Friedman after all. Peter kept mentioning the name Levin, which had been the name of William's father as well. Peter's mother's name was Sidney—Sidney had been William's mother's name before she changed it to Charity. Peter had been told to head for the Delaware River near Philadelphia if he was ever freed; William's mother lived near the Delaware River, on the east side in New Jersey.

William thought of his own mother as he stared hard at Peter. The brow line was nearly identical, and the eyes had a familiar shape. The bridge of the nose was also the same, except that Peter's nose was somewhat broader. The lips were dissimilar, but both had high cheekbones, a trait inherited from ancestral intermarriage with the Lenape Indians.

William Still sat lost in thought. All he'd been told growing up was that his two older "lost brothers" had been sold to an unknown location. His mother had never stopped praying for . . . Levin and Peter.

William was dumbfounded when he heard Peter say the names of his two younger sisters—Mahalah and Kitturah. Mahalah and Kitturah were the very names of William's older sisters who had escaped with their mother long ago.

William Still had been born twenty years after Peter. Nevertheless, how had he not seen the striking resemblance to his, to *their*, mother when Peter first walked into his office? It was so obvious now. William later recalled, "My feelings were unutterable. I could see in the face of my newfound brother, the likeness of my mother."

Very slowly William said, "Suppose I should tell you that I am your brother?" Peter sat there speechless, trying to absorb what he had just heard. The very man sitting across the desk helping him find his family just claimed to be a brother he never even knew existed. Having known nothing but hardship and heartache all his life, Peter was amazed he could have encountered such a stroke of good fortune and was overcome with emotion.

Peter "Still," as he was informed his last name was (their father had changed his last name from "Steel" to "Still"), had never been forgotten by his family after all. Their parents had gone on to have fourteen more children. Their father had died eight years earlier, but their mother was still alive. Their sisters, Mahalah and Kitturah, lived in Philadelphia. Three more of Peter's new siblings lived nearby: Mary ran a school for black children in the city, and James (a doctor) and Samuel (a farmer) both lived in New Jersey. Peter's family had grown exponentially. His mother had eighteen children; eight of whom were still living. All of them were eager to see the older brother about whom they had heard so much.

Peter's reunion with his mother was an answered prayer. Her aged hands trembled as she reached up to hold his still-familiar face. Peter felt his mother's frail embrace, and neither of them could contain their sobs.

The missing pieces of Peter's life came together at what seemed like lightning speed. Peter discovered he had lived in Maryland as a child. On that first escape attempt, his family had made it to New Jersey before being dragged back. His mother had then made the heart-rending decision to escape with his sisters and had never forewarned her sons, in order to protect them. Unable to take all her children with her, she had kissed her sons good-bye as they slept and put them in God's hands. Peter's grandmother had been wise in admonishing Peter to remember that his mother was near the Delaware River. His family was indeed nearby in Burlington, New Jersey.

With the discovery of his mother and siblings, Peter's broken heart was half-filled with joy. The other half ached for his wife and children, who remained in bondage.

Only one week after the reunion, Peter Still returned to the Mc-Kiernon plantation in Tuscumbia, Alabama, where his family lived, carrying $100 that he had raised. His mission now was to try to bring his own wife and children north to meet the rest of his family.

MISSION IMPOSSIBLE
Peter Still's Plan

1851

Seth Concklin had always felt sympathy for the oppressed. He had supported his widowed mother and siblings since the age of fifteen, often aided destitute strangers, and once rescued a man about to be lynched by a mob. It seemed a natural step for this unassuming and sympathetic man to join the growing ranks of the abolition movement. By age forty-eight, he had a perfect record liberating slaves.

Concklin had just read a story in the *Pennsylvania Freeman* that a man named Peter Still had recently been reunited with his mother and siblings after forty-four years of bondage. The man's wife and children still remained enslaved in Alabama. Incited to action, Concklin contacted the Pennsylvania Anti-slavery Society—even though he had never met Peter Still.

Seth Concklin was told by William Still and J. M. McKim, who never consulted the rest of the Vigilance Committee, that agents were not sent south on rescue missions. The purpose of the office was to assist runaways who came to their town. Concklin was not dissuaded.

Peter Still had gone to Tuscumbia, Alabama, in an attempt to free his family himself, but failed. When he returned to Philadelphia, he was informed that a stranger named Seth Concklin had offered to help his family escape. At first Peter was reluctant to accept Concklin's gracious offer, but seeing no other viable option, he finally agreed.

It was decided that once in Alabama, Concklin would assume the name of "John H. Miller," a slave owner traveling north with his slaves. Peter Still explained the layout of the plantation where his family lived and gave descriptions of his wife and children. He gave Concklin a cape that belonged to his wife, Vina (Lavinia), in order to identify Concklin to her as someone to trust. He also passed along the $100 he had earlier raised for his family's release.

In January of 1851 Seth Concklin began exploring possible river routes north from Alabama. He would take the Tennessee River to the Ohio, and then up the Wabash River into Indiana and on to Detroit, where they would cross into Canada.

On a rainy Tuesday in late January, Concklin arrived at McKiernon's plantation, where Peter's family lived, under the pretense of looking for work. With the aid of a slave, he set up a rendezvous with Peter's family. He identified himself to Vina as John H. Miller, and presented his escape plan to her and her three children—twenty-one-year-old Levin, nineteen-year-old Peter, and thirteen-year-old Catharine. (Four other children died young, and a son drowned at age seventeen.) They were to leave in four weeks.

The steamboat schedule along the Tennessee River was unreliable, so Concklin went to Cincinnati to procure a six-oared skiff for their escape. Vina's master, Bernard McKiernon, was on the same steamboat that Concklin took to Cincinnati, totally unaware of the unfolding plot.

Months later, in early March when McKiernon was in New Orleans, Vina and her children met up with "John H. Miller" at 3:00

a.m. on a deserted area along the Tennessee River. They slipped into the waiting skiff, with Peter and Levin taking up the oars beside Concklin. By daybreak they were passing Eastport, Mississippi, where the river turned and headed north through Tennessee. It was just the beginning of a daunting and dangerous six-hundred-mile journey.

At one point during this first leg of the trip, they narrowly missed passing McKiernon's steamboat as he returned from his trip down the Tennessee River to Alabama. Luckily Concklin and the Still family were on the other side of an island in the river.

It was a Sunday in mid-March when the boatload of fugitives noticed another skiff floating toward them down the Tennessee River. Concklin immediately quit the oars and loudly ordered his "slaves" (young Levin and Peter) to row harder. Vina and Catharine hid under blankets, hoping that they had not been found out. On Monday, March 17, fierce winds nearly pushed their skiff toward the riverbank's rocky shore. What should have been a thirty-six-hour trip to the Ohio River had taken fifty-two hours. The Stills could only hope that the close calls and delays thus far were not an omen of things to come.

At sunrise on Tuesday they set up the Ohio River, sixteen hours behind Concklin's time schedule. It was a seventy-five-mile row to the mouth of the Wabash and then another forty-four miles to New Harmony, Indiana, where they landed at 10:00 a.m. on Sunday, March 23. They had been rowing for seven straight days and nights.

Concklin's first concern was to throw off any slave catchers who might be on their trail. Once they left the river, he found clothes more typical of local free blacks than the recognized garments common to slaves. The weary band of fugitives began traveling on public roads to Princeton and Vincennes, Indiana. Over a five-day period, they stayed with various agents of the Underground Railroad prearranged by Concklin.

On Friday, March 28, while walking along the road, nineteen-year-old Peter helped retrieve a runaway spotted horse for its owner. Not long afterward, a man in front of a sawmill tried to start up a conversation by inquiring which way they were traveling. At nightfall the group stopped at another house in Vincennes, Indiana. Concklin went ahead to arrange the next stopping place, having no idea that leaving the Stills would be a costly mistake.

While sitting around a fire, Vina Still and her children heard the sound of horses' hooves outside. Seven men came to the door. One was the owner of the spotted horse young Peter had rescued; another was the man they had spoken to by the sawmill. Vina answered their questions, saying that they had come from Kentucky and were going to Springfield, Illinois. Their master had died, and they'd been left to his brother, John H. Miller, the man with whom they were traveling, but was presently out. The rowdy white men were suspicious, perhaps because of the way the Stills were dressed. Not satisfied with their answers, the men bound the fugitives with rope, put them in a wagon, and hauled them away.

A harried Concklin, returning from making arrangements for their next stop, arrived just as the Stills were being carted away. He raced after the family and overtook them. Concklin climbed into their wagon and began untying them in the dark, but then the ruffians noticed him. A gun was placed to his head and he was ordered to stop. Concklin was lucky he was not apprehended as well.

The dispirited group of fugitives was locked up in the jail in Vincennes, Indiana. Concklin, still believing that he could rescue them, visited them every day, trying to work out a new plan. He had never met with failure before and was determined to return Peter Still's family to him.

In the interim a telegram message was sent out to various regions in the South with a description of the runaways, inquiring if a reward would be offered for their return. Coincidentally, Bernard McKiernon had also sent out a dispatch to the marshal of Evansville describing his runaways and offering a reward of $400 for the return of his "property" and another $600 for the "apprehension of the thief; and his delivery in South Florence, Alabama." Vina well knew being branded as runaways did not bode well for her or her children.

When the abductors learned of the reward, Concklin himself was seized, put in irons, and jailed. A letter sent by Concklin to a friend, asking for bail money, arrived too late to render assistance. McKiernon came to Indiana and identified his slaves, who were then remanded to him without benefit of a formal hearing. He questioned them all. Vina concocted a story in an attempt to protect Concklin, saying that four men had taken them away and delivered them to John H. Miller, aka Concklin. Concklin denied the existence of the four men, insisting that he had acted alone. This incensed McKiernon, who said he would see Concklin hanged in Alabama.

In the morning Seth Concklin, Vina, and her children, Levin, Peter, and Catharine, were all put in a coach and taken to Evansville, Indiana. The prisoners were housed and guarded on the second floor of a private residence. The next morning they were to be sent south on board the steamboat *Paul Anderson*. Concklin, who had slept in a separate chamber away from the runaway slaves, had disappeared overnight. The steamboat was searched, with Vina hoping that he had escaped. It wasn't to be, however.

A letter from the Reverend N. R. Johnson to William Still at the Pennsylvania Anti-slavery Society in Philadelphia dated March 31, 1851, related Seth Concklin's fate. His bludgeoned body was found floating in the river, his head fractured and his irons still on. McKiernon, the last person to have been seen with Concklin, insisted that he must have tried to escape and died in the attempt. Concklin's body was buried still bound in chains. There was no further inquiry into his mysterious death despite the obvious foul play. It was later written that Seth Concklin was "a whole abolition society in himself."

Back in Philadelphia, Peter Still waited for word at his sister's house. It had been eight months since he arrived in Philadelphia, and he desperately wanted his family with him. Soon the devastating news reached Peter regarding Concklin's murder and his family's recapture. The brutal manner of Concklin's death, combined with the story of his daring rescue mission, did much to bolster support for the Still family's release. Peter Still made an appeal to purchase his wife and three children from McKiernon. In August 1851 McKiernon replied, offering to sell them for the exorbitant sum of $5,000: $1,000 per person, and another $1,000 for his trouble in capturing them from Concklin.

Peter Still began traveling and speaking tirelessly at abolitionist meetings, telling his tragic tale. He learned to read and write and received assistance penning his life story, *The Kidnapped and the Ransomed*. It took four years to raise the money to purchase his family's freedom.

On New Year's Eve 1854, Peter Still was reunited with his family in Cincinnati, Ohio. Vina and his three children were brought to New Jersey, where they were warmly welcomed by the extended family of William Still, Peter's long-lost brother with whom he had been reunited four years earlier. Peter Still enjoyed fourteen years of freedom living on a ten-acre farm in Burlington, New Jersey, with his family until his death in 1868 at age sixty-eight.

The Still clan, of which there are now more than three thousand members, continues the tradition set in 1870 of holding family reunions. Family ties, though once severed, still remain strong.

UP A TREE
Charles Gilbert,
Higee Hotel Resident

1854

With only seconds to think, Charles Gilbert got up on all fours in the dark and began growling and barking like a mad dog. Even he was surprised by the terrifying sounds emanating from his own throat. An intruder had entered the dark confines of the young man's hiding place beneath the foundation of a stately hotel, and Charles was literally barking to save his life.

In 1854 Charles Gilbert was living in Richmond, Virginia, one of the largest slave-trading centers on the East Coast. His master, Benjamin Davis, was a notorious slave trader always looking to make a profit. Charles had suffered under Davis and was not saddened to learn he was about to be sold. However, after ads had run for months in the newspapers, there had been no takers. Davis had been convinced he could get a good price for Gilbert. His fine build, his intelligent look, and his "ginger-bread color" were all assets that would help him command a handsome sum.

While Davis tried to find a buyer, Charles tried to find out how to run away. A sympathetic schooner captain from Boston was rumored to take fugitives as passengers for a price. After making the necessary inquiries, Charles learned that if he could make it from Richmond to Old Point Comfort on Virginia's east coast, he could be smuggled aboard for a fee of $30. Charles first needed to make it to the James River, which emptied into the Chesapeake Bay, roughly eighty miles distant.

In late July, Charles Gilbert left. Davis immediately had slave catchers on his trail. He knew that Charles had family in Old Point Comfort, where he lived as a young boy. Slave catchers arrived ahead of Charles and began threatening his family. Word quickly spread around town: Anyone assisting Charles would suffer greatly for it.

Davis put up a $200 reward for Charles's capture. Only one brave friend in Old Point Comfort, identified only as E. S., defiantly took Charles in for a week, putting his own safety in jeopardy. The slave hunters' intimidation worked, and Charles had nowhere else to go.

Charles decided to hide out under the Higee Hotel. The hotel's large frame was supported on wooden piers, creating an expansive crawlspace underneath. The dark, musty place was home to chickens and other animals that scurried about. Left with no other choice, Charles took refuge in the dank filth under the hotel.

Gilbert made his bed next to the cistern that held the hotel's water supply. For four weeks, in filthy and cramped living quarters, he survived on the hotel's garbage. He did not dare venture out until the slave hunters had left town. But one evening an unexpected intruder crawled under the hotel with him. Charles lay flat on the ground. In the dark shadows he could make out the form of a small boy innocently searching for chickens. If the boy came much closer to the cistern, Charles would be discovered.

Immediately Charles crouched on his bent arms and legs and barked ferociously. The terrified youngster clambered out as fast as he could. Charles was satisfied with his quick thinking until he overheard the boy's father say he would come back and kill the mad dog.

Charles left that very night, walking over ten miles to Bay Shore near Virginia Beach, where he hid in the woods. He concealed himself in the thick underbrush, but at daybreak could see that the cover was insufficient. He climbed high up a giant tree and nestled himself securely between the V-shaped branches. Charles sat for an entire day watching people pass below him as he racked his brains trying to figure out where to go next.

He made his way back to a poor washerwoman in Old Point Comfort named Isabella who took in boarders, hoping she might sympathize with the downtrodden. Seeing his desperate situation, she agreed to hide him under the floorboards of her house. Charles's friend John Thomas was the only other person who knew of the arrangement. Charles stayed in this underground sanctuary for two weeks, waiting for the search to die down. Meanwhile he could hear the voices of Isabella and his friend talking through the floorboards.

At one point six officers arrived, tramping through the house and accusing Isabella of hiding Davis's runaway. One of the men offered John Thomas $25 for any information, but both Thomas and Isabella claimed to know nothing about the missing slave's whereabouts.

This close encounter with being recaptured prompted Charles to go back to the Higee Hotel for another week, thus relieving his friends of the danger in which they had put themselves. Afterward he left for the isolated forested area located behind the cottage of a man named Stephen Allen. Charles hoped to find some impenetrable hiding places in the dense thicket. The next day the old man drew close, so Gilbert once again barked ferociously from the underbrush, and the old man hobbled off.

Slave hunters were still actively searching the area around Richmond, Petersburg, and Old Point Comfort. Desperation made

Charles take refuge in a marsh near the Great Dismal Swamp. This turned out to be a poor choice due to the stench, the mosquitoes, and the snakes that lived there. After just two hours he returned to the Higee Hotel for a third time.

After a two-day stay under the hotel, Charles appealed to his mother, Margaret Johnson, for help. She had purchased her freedom, but all four of her sons were still enslaved. She finally could no longer stand to see her son in such a dire situation. No matter the risk, she vowed to help him.

Margaret had saved a little bit of money, and she gave it to her son. He now had enough money to pay his way on board a vessel heading for Philadelphia, Pennsylvania, where he'd heard the Anti-slavery Society assisted all runaways.

Charles Gilbert had just one more day and night in Virginia before his ship to freedom left port. He went back to the old washerwoman's house to clean up and spend his last hours there. He had intended to stay under Isabella's floorboards, but after three hours the coast seemed clear. It had been so long since he'd had any semblance of comfort, and he was exhausted from the stress of constantly being on the run. He went upstairs to rest in an empty bedroom, which obviously belonged to a female boarder, as it was full of garments and luggage.

Suddenly a pounding came on the front door of the house. Three officers insisted on searching the premises. While questioning Isabella about her boarders, she attempted to stall as best she could. Meanwhile one of the officers tramped upstairs, opening the door to the room Charles had entered.

Charles stepped out from behind a curtained wall that served as a room divider and strolled right past the officer, walking like a girl down the stairs in an old calico dress and bonnet, completely done up in women's attire. Isabella did not blink an eye.

The officer inquired, "Whose gal are you?" Charles's entire future, his precious freedom, depended on not just his answer, but on his elevated, evenly pitched, feminine voice. Exuding confidence, Charles nonchalantly replied, "Mr. Cockling's, sir." When asked her name, he replied, "Delie, sir." After what may have seemed like an eternity, the officer offered up the sweetest three words Charles Gilbert had ever heard: "Go on then!" Charles walked right out of the washhouse to begin his new life.

Charles Gilbert paid a $30 fee and boarded the vessel for Philadelphia. Disappointed to learn that it was not a direct route, he was forced to take cover during a four-week layover in Norfolk, Virginia. By that time the reward Davis had posted in the Richmond newspapers for his capture had increased to $550. When the steamer finally pulled into Philadelphia on November 11, 1854, Davis's men were still searching for him back in Virginia.

Like many travelers on the Underground Railroad, Charles Gilbert's journey to freedom was impossibly difficult. Yet after three and a half months, his endurance was rewarded as he finally attained freedom.

DOWNRIVER
John Fairfield's Fury

Mid-1850s

John Fairfield was a man possessed. He angrily pulled on his boots, grabbed his whip, and stormed out of his cabin. News that one of his two slaves had escaped was bad enough, but hearing that his boat was also missing infuriated him. He stomped down to the saltworks along West Virginia's Kanawha River, demanding that his remaining slave be summoned. In front of a gathering crowd, Fairfield accused the frightened man of being involved in the disappearance. He cracked his whip near the slave's head, ignoring the man's repeated denials of wrongdoing.

Fairfield had recently learned that the water along the Kanawha River was saturated with salt. Since the early 1800s more than 1,250 pounds of salt had been extracted every day. The wealthy businessman viewed the salt trade as a lucrative investment. He took his two best slaves and went to investigate, hoping to haul the salt downriver and sell it for a sizable profit.

Fairfield arrived in Charleston, West Virginia, and came to know the local slaveholders along the Kanawha River. He contracted the building of two boats to transport his salt and gleaned what he could about the business. While waiting for the construction to be completed, Fairfield commiserated with fellow slaveholders on the difficulties of managing their slaves.

On a Saturday night after the first boat was completed, one of Fairfield's slaves joined up with a local slave who had knowledge of boating. They crept down to the river under a dark moonless sky. The men slowly untied the rope on Fairfield's boat and listened intently for any sounds. When the coast seemed clear, the men pushed off and headed downriver, letting the swift spring current carry them along. After some distance they steered the boat to the bank and threw a line to the men who appeared out of the brush.

Quickly the boat was filled to capacity with fugitive slaves. Not a sound was uttered by any of the men, women, and children who crouched down to hide their heads from view. The boat drifted along the Kanawha River, beginning its sixty-mile journey to the Ohio River and freedom.

The next day the slave owners noticed the missing slaves. They initiated a thorough frantic search, but it proved fruitless. On Monday morning Fairfield's boat was also discovered missing. The slaveholders assumed that their slaves had stolen his boat in order to escape, and took off on their horses in hot pursuit. When the horsemen reached the mouth of the Ohio River, they found Fairfield's boat beached on the opposite side. The slaves were long gone.

When John Fairfield heard about his boat being stolen, he put fear in the men in camp. He demanded retribution. Not only was he out a considerable amount of money, but he was livid that his slave had most likely run off with the others. As his second boat neared completion, Fairfield vowed to watch his remaining slave, whom he greatly distrusted, like a hawk.

The following Saturday night, Fairfield's other slave absconded with his second boat, taking an additional ten or twelve slaves with him. How they managed to slip away under Fairfield's watchful eye remained a mystery to the slaveholders in Charleston.

When Fairfield was informed that his second boat and slave were missing, his fury knew no bounds. He exploded in a burst of uncontrollable anger, ranting and raving that he was now ruined. This time Fairfield joined the other men on horseback and set off, determined to capture the slaves. They rode sixty miles in hot pursuit, only to be disappointed. There on the other side of the Ohio River was Fairfield's second boat, empty of slaves. The unspoken fear was that the fugitive slaves had been forwarded along the circuitous path of Ohio's well-established Underground Railroad.

The men crossed the Ohio River and followed Fairfield's suggestion to split up in order to widen their search. When the pursuers later met at the designated rendezvous point to confer on their findings, Fairfield was not present. He had disappeared. It was probably some time before the slaveholders realized they had been outwitted.

Fairfield was not the pro-slavery Virginian he claimed to be. What the Kanawha-area slaveholders didn't realize was that Fairfield, the self-important businessman, was not from Louisville, Kentucky, at all, nor was he using his real name of John Fairfield. He had given the Kanawha slaveholders an alias. And the "slave" whom Fairfield had berated and frightened with his whip was all an act. The two slaves Fairfield had brought with him were actually free men from Ohio—relatives of those they had come to rescue.

John Fairfield was born into a slave-owning family from Virginia, but eventually came to disagree with his family's position on slavery. As an adult he helped a childhood friend, Bill, escape bondage from his uncle's farm. From that point on, Fairfield realized that liberating slaves was possible if one possessed a sense of adventure, a willingness to take risks, and a cunning mind.

By the 1850s, word of Fairfield's daring exploits in assisting fugitive slaves had spread up North, and the demand for his services grew accordingly. He was especially passionate about reuniting families separated by slavery. The methods Fairfield used to rescue slaves were viewed as controversial by fellow abolitionists. Fairfield's response to such criticism was, "Slaveholders are all devils, and it is no harm to kill the devil. I do not intend to hurt people if they keep out of the way, but if they step in between me and liberty, they must take the consequences. When I undertake to conduct slaves out of bondage I feel that it is my duty to defend them, even to the last drop of my blood."

John Fairfield had been approached several times by the freed slaves in Ohio to rescue their loved ones left behind, who toiled at the saltworks along the Kanawha River, near present-day Malden. When he finally agreed to help, he knew he would need an elaborate plan to move such a large number of people. It had taken Fairfield a long time to ingratiate himself with the Kanawha slaveholders and gain the confidence of the influential salt proprietors. While his boats were being built, the "slaves" Fairfield had brought with him were secretly seeking out their relatives to inform them of the escape plan.

Sometimes it would take John Fairfield six months to assume a new role, establish himself in a community, and gain people's confidence. He was so convincing in the roles he assumed and the false pretenses he arranged that he was rarely implicated. Fairfield masterminded countless schemes, posing as a slave trader, a slaveholder, or a businessman using different aliases every time. Once he donned the attire of an undertaker and led twenty-eight slaves to freedom in a staged funeral procession as they carried an empty coffin right out of town.

The peace-loving Quaker abolitionist Levi Coffin shared these words about John Fairfield: "With all his faults and misguided impulses, and wicked ways, he was a brave man; he never betrayed a trust that was reposed in him, and he was a true friend to the oppressed and suffering slave."

Though fellow abolitionists did not always condone Fairfield's methods of arming his fugitives and using violence if necessary, they did admire his determination. Over a twelve-year period, Fairfield reunited families with their loved ones from Louisiana, Alabama, Georgia, Mississippi, Tennessee, Kentucky, Missouri, and West Virginia. In all he helped to free several thousand slaves, forwarding most of them to Canada via the Underground Railroad. John Fairfield accepted whatever pay was offered to cover his expenses, but his true reward was witnessing the joyful reunion of family members.

Although his final fate is uncertain, it is likely that Fairfield died tragically during a slave insurrection in Tennessee. He fit the description of an unknown white male, new to an area on the Cumberland River, who was killed in a failed escape attempt of a large number of slaves. After 1861 he was never heard from again.

WHERE TO, SIR?
Ann Maria Weems,
Teenage Freedom-Seeker

1855

Ann Maria Weems's family was part slave and part free. By law, even though their father was free, all six of the Weems children took on the slave status of their mother. Three of her brothers had been sold down South, but the Anti-slavery Society gave her father money to buy freedom for two of her brothers. Abolitionist attorney Jacob Bigelow had raised $1,000 to buy her mother's freedom and $1,600 to buy one of her sister's freedom. Ann Maria prayed she would be next, but it wasn't meant to be.

Charles Price owned Ann Maria, and he had no intention of accepting money in exchange for her freedom. Master Price was especially fond of his teenage slave girls. Thirteen-year-old Ann Maria had reason to be afraid. Mr. Bigelow, the lawyer who had taken interest in the Weems family, had tried for two years to purchase her freedom. But even though Ann Maria's master had been offered $700 for her, he had refused. After two years it became clear to Mr. Bigelow that Ann Maria would have to be taken on the Underground Railroad.

For six weeks Ann Maria Weems, now fifteen, slept fretfully in the corner of her master's bedroom. How foolish she'd been to think that she was receiving a privilege when told she would be sleeping in the main house. She feared that Master and Mistress Price were suspicious she might be planning on running away. Why else would they have made her sleep on their bedroom floor? Ann Maria pulled her blanket tight around her shoulders and prayed they did not know any of the details.

Jacob Bigelow, an abolitionist attorney with connections who lived fifteen miles away in Washington, DC, had exchanged a series of letters with William Still in Philadelphia. To work out the logistics of the escape plan, Bigelow had secret meetings with agents whose true identities even he did not know. Somehow he needed to get Ann Maria to the nation's capital, and then he could make arrangements to forward her north. Though Washington, DC, was only fifteen miles from where Ann Maria lived in Rockville, Maryland, it seemed an impossible distance to cover undetected.

Nonetheless, on Sunday night, September 23, 1855, Ann Maria was secreted away, with the assistance of two older cousins who were hoping that Mr. Bigelow might help them escape next. In early October, when it seemed safe to continue on, she arrived in Washington, DC. No one suspected that the respected lawyer Jacob Bigelow, with offices on East and Seventh Streets, and who served on the board of directors of the Washington Gas Light Company, was an agent on the Underground Railroad, running a route through Montgomery County, Maryland, to the District of Columbia.

Using the name William Penn, Bigelow wrote in code to William Still in Philadelphia about a "small package" and said "merchandize shall be delivered" to William Wright, an underground agent in York Springs, Pennsylvania.

While plans were being finalized, slave catchers came to DC looking for Ann Maria Weems. Her master, Charles Price, had offered a $500 reward for her capture, but no fifteen-year-old slave girl fitting her description could be found. Nobody, however, was looking for a fifteen-year-old boy.

Disguised as a coachman named "Joe Wright," Ann Maria donned a boy's black pants and white shirt, a vest, jacket, and neat bow tie. Her hair was cropped, and she wore a cap pulled down low to hide some facial freckles. Young Joe looked the perfect part of a gentleman's coach driver. Ann Maria had been schooled as to how a carriage driver should walk, talk, and act. She was determined to follow every directive down to the minutest detail—her freedom depended upon it.

Ann Maria's escape out of Price's farm in Rockville had initially been hurried, but now she had nothing to do but wait. Time needed to pass in order for her master's slave catchers to give up the chase. Only then would she be taken out of hiding and forwarded on. After six weeks of hiding Ann Maria in the nation's capital, the storm had passed and Bigelow felt safer conducting her to the next stop.

The rendezvous with underground agents would begin right in the center of Washington, DC, where the young coachman, Joe Wright, would be hidden in plain sight. Ann Maria had been told about the white pillars and steps of one of the most famous private residences in the world, the White House, where President Franklin Pierce lived. The open fields that provided pasturage for sheep and cattle, the Treasury Building, and the wooden-domed Capitol had all been described to her. She was not to take any note of them, for gawking like a tourist would only draw unwanted attention. Joe

Wright was to keep his head down as if he drove carriages to and from the District of Columbia every day.

Arrangements were made for Ann Maria to travel with "Dr. H." in late November. Bigelow did not know the man's real name. On the appointed day the esteemed Jacob Bigelow, Esq., and his young coachman, Joe Wright, set out. They had decided to rendezvous with their horse and buggy in a very public place—directly in front of the White House. The city was abuzz with people going in and out of the Treasury Building and the State, War, and Navy Buildings on the brisk fall afternoon. It did not seem out of the ordinary that an unattended horse and buggy should be tied up in front of the White House on Pennsylvania Avenue.

Dr. H. confidently climbed inside the carriage. At that moment Mr. Bigelow and the young coachman walked up. Joe Wright tipped his cap to Dr. H. while the two older gentlemen shook hands. Without further ado, the young driver unhitched the horses from the hitching post, climbed into the seat, took the reins, and drove off. Jacob Bigelow's work was done.

The good Dr. H. took the reins when they were alone on the country roads and put his young charge at ease. They would travel together through several counties in Maryland, along the eastern Pennsylvania border, and on to Philadelphia. It would be necessary to find lodging for a night. Dr. H. told "Joe" that he would look up an old acquaintance and inquire if they could spend the evening on their first night's journey.

Dr. H.'s friends were quite glad to see him and insisted that they accommodate him overnight. When asked why he had come this way after being absent so long, Dr. H. explained that he had not been well and determined that a good drive in the country air might be beneficial to his health.

Joe Wright listened from the kitchen as the adults visited in the parlor. Dr. H. put on all sorts of airs and talked on a variety of subjects, ever ready to agree heartily with his friends' pro-slavery sentiments. Joe Wright knew his place and acted as he had been instructed.

At bedtime Dr. H. suggested his boy remain with him during the night, as his vertigo caused dizzy spells. The friends found the request understandable and made arrangements. In actuality Dr. H. felt safer with his charge not being out of his sight during the evening. Slave catchers may have followed them, or her disguise as a boy might be found out if she was with others. Once again Ann Maria found herself with a blanket on the floor while her "master" slept nearby.

By morning the good doctor was on his way, with his devoted coachman at the reins. At long last they arrived in the free state of Pennsylvania and reached the home of William Still in Philadelphia at 4:00 p.m. on November 25—Thanksgiving Day. The second leg of their journey complete.

William Still was expecting their arrival, but he was not at home. Dr. H. greeted Mrs. Still and told her that he was most anxious to hurry home. He stated, "I wish to leave this young lad with you a short while, and I will call and see further about him." With no good-byes Dr. H. left and was never seen again.

Joe Wright sat nervously in the kitchen in the company of several people: Mrs. Still, a hired girl, and a female runaway slave. When William Still returned home, he was elated to see the disguised coach girl and greeted her accordingly: "I suppose you are the person that the doctor went to Washington after, are you not?" But the young coachman insisted that his name was Joe Wright from York, Pennsylvania, and that he was a servant traveling with the doctor. Still replied, "The doctor went expressly to Washington after a young girl, who was to be brought away dressed up as a boy, and I took you to be the person."

The boy's insistence that he was not that person perplexed William Still, who did not find out the reason for the denial until the two were alone. Ann Maria had been under strict orders not to reveal her true identity to anyone but Mr. Still. In the presence of Mrs. Still and the others, Ann Maria had been taking every precaution not to give herself away.

After several days' rest in Philadelphia, Ann Maria, still disguised as Joe Wright, continued her journey by coach to New York City. Lewis Tappan, an elderly abolitionist in Brooklyn, paid $300 for her transport.

In New York, Reverend Freeman, a black minister, was to accompany "Joe Wright" on the remainder of the journey. The two boarded a train for a three-day ride from New York City to Canada. The long train trip was fraught with worry, as there was now a sizable reward being offered for Charles Price's runaway slave. It wasn't until they passed into Canada that Ann Maria felt safe.

In December of 1855, a full two months and four hundred miles from where she had started, Ann Maria Weems arrived in Chatham, Canada. The fourth and final phase of her journey took her on a twenty-mile carriage ride to the home of her aunt and uncle, the Bradleys in Dresden, where she was finally free to resume her true identity.

Ann Maria was educated forty-five minutes away at the reputable Buxton Mission School in the Elgin Settlement, a cooperative colony for refugees in Canada. By 1858 all six of the children in the Weems family had finally won their freedom. In 1861, when Ann Maria was twenty-one years old, her parents and two youngest siblings moved to Canada for nine years before returning to Washington, DC. After 1861, however, all records of Ann Maria Weems's life are lost to time. Perhaps she permanently changed her name to ensure no trace of her could ever be found.

Ann Maria's former master, Charles Price, had lost one of his favorite slaves, but he ensured countless others did not escape. Several years after Ann Maria's escape, he bought a building with adjoining jail cells on Duke Street in Alexandria, Virginia—a slave-trading pen known as Price, Birch & Co.—which brought terror to anyone held there who awaited his or her doom.

NOT MY CHILD
Margaret Garner's
Heart-Wrenching Decision

1856

The young mother looked down into the pleading and terrified eyes of her little ones. They clutched the folds of her skirt, holding on for dear life as chaos broke out all around them. Glass was breaking, doors were being battered down, and gunshots were going off. There was no escape. Before she knew it, Margaret Garner had done the unthinkable. How had everything gone so wrong?

Margaret Garner and her family and friends had been planning to make a run for freedom for some time. She was part of a group of seventeen slaves owned by Archibald K. Gaines and John Marshall of Boone County, Kentucky, not far from the free soil of Ohio. Their plan was to wait until winter and then head to the frozen Ohio River and walk across. Margaret, who may have been expecting again, and her husband, Robert, were accompanied by their four children, two boys and two girls, as well as her elderly in-laws, Simon and Mary Garner. The youngest was a daughter just several months old.

It was a freezing cold night on January 27, 1856, when the group set out. They stole two horses and a sled from one of the master's barns and quietly led the horses past the slave quarters. All seventeen bundled up as best they could and climbed into the sled. Horses' hooves clopped and sled runners whispered over snow. If caught, they would be charged not only with horse theft but with absconding with their owner's other property—the sled and themselves.

It was not yet dawn when they arrived at Covington, Kentucky, across from an area called Western Row on the Ohio River. The group tied up the horses and slipped over the frozen river to Ohio. To avoid attracting attention, they decided to disperse into the streets of Cincinnati. The slaves separated into two groups and went their own way, with hoods and scarves covering their faces and heads bent low out of the blustery winds.

The nine slaves who had belonged to John Marshall went uptown, seeking out safe houses. They would stay the night in Cincinnati before being safely forwarded along the Underground Railroad to Canada.

Archibald K. Gaines's eight slaves that made up the Garner family asked for directions to the home of Elijah Kite, a free black kinsman who lived a few miles from the river. They found a safe haven there and warmed themselves by the fire as they discussed the next course of action. They knew full well that Gaines and Marshall were already pursuing them.

After feeding the Garners, Elijah Kite went to the office of Levi Coffin, just a half-mile away, seeking advice. Coffin, the well-known President of the Underground Railroad, told Kite to move the Garners immediately to Mill Creek, a black community outside of the city. From Mill Creek, arrangements would be made to move them along the Underground Railroad.

Elijah Kite returned with the good news, only to find his house surrounded by a posse of men, including Archibald Gaines, John

Marshall, and a US marshal and his deputy. Gaines demanded that the slaves inside Kite's house surrender. All hopes of escape were seemingly dashed. It had only taken a few hours for Gaines and Marshall to discover their slaves were missing, and they had traced their path in the snow to Cincinnati. A few more inquiries directed them to Kite's home.

Margaret Garner had come so close to setting her four children free. She wasn't going to give up her hopes so easily. She and the other adults barred the doors and windows; grabbed knives, clubs, and guns; and vowed to die fighting rather than be taken back to slavery. One of the windows shattered, spraying glass across the floor.

The screams of children pierced the air. There was no time to think, only act. Outside in the yard, Deputy Marshal John Patterson was grazed by a bullet fired from inside the house. The door was rammed and nearly broken off its hinges. In the chaos Margaret Garner declared that she would rather kill her children and herself than return to slavery. As the door broke down, her husband shot off his pistol, wounding one of the men before he himself was overpowered.

In the noise and confusion, Margaret looked down at her beautiful three-year-old daughter, Mary. The little child would now have to endure the same degradation and horrors that many enslaved women like Margaret suffered in submitting to their masters. She wanted to save her from the same agony.

Before she quite knew what she was doing, Margaret Garner had taken a knife and slit the throat of her dear daughter. In the confusion of the fighting around her, she then attempted to take a shovel and beat her four-year-old and six-year-old sons over the head. She would save them from the evils of slavery as well.

Margaret's elderly mother-in-law witnessed the horrible scene but did not intervene, either stunned into inaction—or perhaps understanding she might have done the same under similar circumstances. Elijah Kite's wife disarmed Margaret, and one of the men overpowered her before she could take her own life. The distraught young mother fell to the floor, sobbing. She cried that "she would rather kill every one of her children than have them taken back across the river." Margaret's daughter soon died. Her two sons, while bloody, were without serious injury. The infant was bruised in the melee but survived.

The Garner family was apprehended and brought before a US District Court in Cincinnati. They offered barely audible answers to a barrage of questions. When asked about an old scar across the side of her face, Margaret answered dully, "White man struck me." When it was suggested that she had gone insane in killing her own daughter, Margaret answered quite clearly, "No, I was as cool as I now am, and would much rather kill them at once, and thus end their sufferings, than have them taken back to slavery and be murdered by piecemeal."

A stunned nation read the headlines in the newspapers on January 28, 1856. The *New York Times* printed a telegram received from Cincinnati: "A stampede of slaves from the border counties of Kentucky took place last night. One slave woman finding escape, cut the throats of her children, and severely wounded others." Readers grappled with the unimaginable concept of a mercy killing. What would possess a mother to take the life of her own child? Could slavery truly be so evil?

Margaret Garner was arrested in Cincinnati on a criminal charge of murder, and her husband and parents were arrested for complicity in murder. The Garner trial lasted two weeks. The Garners' lawyers, Jolliffe and Getchell, intended to prevent the Garners from being returned to their master. At first they argued that since the Garners had previously been brought to Ohio by their owner, they were technically free at the time they had tried to escape. US Commissioner John Pendry, who was hearing the case, overruled that argument. He found that if the Garners had voluntarily returned to the slave state of Kentucky, they had relinquished their claim to freedom.

Jolliffe next wanted the state to have his clients arrested for murder, which would prevent their return to Kentucky—and the clutches of their master, Archibald Gaines. He was fully confident that no court would find the young mother guilty, for she had heartily believed it better to free her children's souls than have them endure a life of slavery. A jury would certainly be sympathetic to her plight.

In the end, the rights of the slave owners prevailed over the right of the state of Ohio to seek punishment for murder. Abolitionists appealed to Ohio governor Salmon P. Chase, who supported the state's claim that the fugitives were free people, but even he could not prevent the Garners' return to slavery. The state's writ of habeas corpus compelling the Garners to be brought before the court was ignored by the US marshal. Five weeks after the incident, the Garners were remanded to Archibald Gaines, who then sold them to the Deep South.

As if there had not already been enough tragedy in their family, the ship transporting the Garners had an accident at sea. In the collision some of the slaves who were in chains were hurled overboard. Margaret Garner, with her infant in her arms, either fell into the water or jumped. She was saved, but the baby was drowned. As Margaret saw it, two of her children had now been rescued from a doomed life of slavery.

While some found Margaret Garner's actions to be barbaric, others found them noble. In either case, the public was forced to consider the cruel effects of slavery, both physical and psychological. Margaret was never set free until her own death a few years later in 1858 from typhoid fever. She was about twenty-five years old.

Ohio-born author Toni Morrison was moved by Margaret Garner's horrifying ordeal. Her 1987 Pulitzer Prize–winning novel *Beloved* found seeds of inspiration in certain aspects of the young mother's tragic life.

FREEDOM TRAIN
John Thompson's Railroad

1857

For the first time in his life, nineteen-year-old John Thompson felt free. As the train pulled out of the Alabama train depot, the night wind blew refreshingly cool on his skin. While the train chugged north, the passengers looking out the windows were treated to a blue moon landscape under a star-studded sky. Thompson, however, had the best view—he was riding on top of the train.

For John, it was high time to escape. He was born in Fauquier County, Virginia, in 1838 and had grown up forty miles east, in Alexandria. For as long as he could remember, he had answered to a master. The last time John Thompson had seen any of his siblings was when he was five years old. They had been sold to various owners, making it impossible for him to keep connected to his family.

His earliest memory was of being sold away from his mother, Matilda Tate, and taken from his home in Virginia to North Carolina. In the years afterward, it seemed as if John was sold whenever a master thought there was money to be made off of him. He finally ended up in Huntsville, Alabama, on a cotton plantation belonging to Hezekiah Thompson. While John took on his master's surname, that was all he had in common with the man.

Hezekiah Thompson was a cruel master. The profitability of his plantation crop depended on having his slaves work harder than was humanly possible. Master Thompson was a young man "fond of drinking and carousing, and always ready for a fight or a knock-down." John decided to make a break for freedom after being beaten so severely with a bullwhip that his arm was rendered useless for half a week.

For two years he had toiled endlessly in Alabama cotton fields for Hezekiah Thompson, watching trains pass by. At last he came up with a plan to ride north to freedom on one of those passing trains one way or another.

John escaped under the cover of night, making his way to the train depot. When all the ticketed passengers were on board, the conductor signaled the engineer, and the train slowly lurched out of the station. John hid in some brush by the tracks. When the train began to accelerate, he ran alongside, pulling himself up and scrambling unnoticed to the roof of one of the cars. He lay flat, hanging onto the roof as his heart beat furiously. The sensation of freedom was thrilling.

John had no other plan than to scramble on and off trains, riding at night, and hiding and sleeping during the day. Somehow he had to find out which trains would take him from Alabama back to his childhood home in Alexandria, Virginia, where he hoped he could see his mother again. John had no knowledge of geography. He would have to rely on overhearing people's conversations in the train station. He thought perhaps he could masquerade as someone's valet, getting luggage, but soon noticed he did not have the appropriate attire. He had to resort to hiding in the underbrush near the track and listening as the conductors yelled out the train destinations.

For more than six hundred miles and over the course of two weeks, the determined young man fought fear, hunger, and exhaustion as he traveled home toward Alexandria. Each peaceful night ride through the countryside abruptly ended with the screech of brakes and a billow of steam from the engine, which thankfully helped to conceal him at times as he scurried from the train. Under the cover of darkness, John would jump off and disappear into the brush to wait out the day and forage for food. He also had to be wary of slave patrollers looking for runaways.

Finally John reached Richmond, Virginia, a slave-trading center. He knew Richmond was not safe due to the many slave chasers in the area. He intended to leave the city, making his way to Alexandria as quickly as possible.

Unfortunately, after two short weeks of freedom, he was found out and apprehended. Without free papers, John was put in prison and his master, Hezekiah Thompson, was sent for. Word reached John's mother, Matilda, that he was back in the state. She visited him in jail, overjoyed to see her son, yet saddened at the occasion. While it broke his heart to see his mother distressed, John reassured her that better days lay ahead.

Hezekiah Thompson came up north to claim John, at first intending to take him back to Alabama to "make an example of him." He soon changed his mind, however, and put John up on the auction block.

A Richmond slave trader named Green McMurray bought John for $1,300. McMurray saw great promise in him, and planned to put him up for resale immediately. But there were no takers due to the inflated asking price and hard times.

John Thompson was still determined to have his freedom. The train he went looking for the next time, however, was on the Underground Railroad. Many escape routes had their junctions in Virginia, and a well-organized system of "lines" led out of the city. He escaped from Green McMurray and made his way back to Alexandria, where he saw his mother once again. He had six brothers and sisters, some of whom he had not seen since he was five years old.

In October of 1857 John Thompson, together with a man from Charleston, South Carolina, named William Cooper, found their way to Philadelphia, to the Pennsylvania Anti-slavery Society, whose secretary, William Still, was said to assist any fugitive slave who found their office.

William Still listened attentively to Thompson's story, marveling at his creative mode of escape. The Vigilance Committee then assisted both John Thompson and William Cooper by forwarding them farther north.

Settled in Syracuse, New York, John wrote to his mother, "I hird when I was on the Underground R. Road that the Hounds was on my track but it was no go. I new I was too far out of their Reach where they would never smell my track." He had learned the trade of barbering and set up shop with a friend. "I am getting $12 per month for what Little work I am Doing." Compared to picking cotton, being a barber surely must not have seemed like hard labor.

John Thompson was content and did quite well for two years. However, his former master, Green McMurray, had not forgiven him for running away. Someone betrayed John, and he learned just in time that McMurray was in town, searching for him. Fearing recapture, Thompson immediately took leave of the city and set sail for London, far from the grasp of slaveholders. He arrived across the Atlantic in December of 1860.

There is no record that John Thompson was ever reunited with his mother, or even if he returned to the United States after slavery was abolished in 1865. Perhaps his mother was comforted by a letter he had once written her in which he claimed:

> *I am now a free man Living By the sweet of my own*
> *Brow not serving a nother man & giving him all I Earn*
> *But what I make is mine and iff one Plase do not sute*
> *me I am at Liberty to Leave and go some where elce &*
> *can ashore you I think highly of Freedom and would not*
> *exchange it for nothing that is offered me for it.*

IN THE DARK OF NIGHT
Arnold Gragston's Freedom Boat

1859

Fifteen-year-old Arnold Gragston slowly pushed the skiff away from shore, being careful not to let the bottom scrape on the beach. Even in the dark of night, Arnold and the girl he was with hunkered down low in the boat. He silently pulled the oars through the water, working against the current. Arnold's arms trembled from the strain. He would have loved to have looked into the gorgeous brown eyes of his sweet passenger, but he settled instead for feeling her eyes upon him.

A life lived in slavery or in freedom could be decided by as little as which side of the river you were born on. A slave in Kentucky only needed to cross the Ohio River to reach Ohio's free soil. Arnold Gragston had never considered daring to cross himself, but one night he was asked to do it for someone else. Just the thought of it terrified him.

Arnold Gragston lived on Walton Pike in Mason County, Kentucky. Born on Christmas Day in the early 1840s, he was one of ten slaves belonging to Colonel John "Jack" Tabb, whose farm was between Germantown and Minerva. Arnold found Master Tabb to be a "pretty good man," as he gave relatively few beatings. He permitted his slaves to be taught to read, write, and figure, even though fellow farm owners looked down on educating slaves. Tabb also did what he could to see that husbands and wives either worked on the same farm or, at the very least, lived together at the end of the day.

Arnold was a quick learner and was often hired out by Colonel Tabb to other farms. Consequently, he had freedom to travel during the day, which made him familiar with the surrounding area. He was also allowed quite a bit of liberty at night, which meant that he could "go a-courtin'." Little did Arnold know that his courting on one particular night would lead him to become part of a network that helped liberate slaves.

One evening in 1859 Arnold headed out to a nearby farm to call upon a pretty girl. Arnold was slight of build and not very tall, but he had spruced himself up to make a good impression. The old woman who answered the door, however, had plans other than accepting suitors. She explained to Arnold that she wanted him to row the girl across the river to Ohio.

Arnold was taken aback by the request, and his mind churned with the dangers inherent in such a mission. Too frightened to speak, he began to take his leave, but then the girl came to the door. She was "such a pretty little thing—brown-skinned and kinda rosy and looking as scared as I was feelin'." The young Arnold Gragston was fixated and couldn't help but listen as the old woman laid out the details of the escape. The young girl's eyes betrayed how frightened she was.

No matter how smitten, Arnold just could not bring himself to take such a risk without first mulling it over. As hard as it was to believe, the grandmother claimed there were white folks in Ohio who actually helped slaves escape. He only needed to get the girl to the other side of the river. Arnold had no peace of mind that night as he envisioned himself undergoing the lash at the hands of an enraged master or, worse yet, being shot and killed for his part in a foiled escape attempt.

Tabb's farm, where Arnold lived, was six miles directly south of Dover, Kentucky, a tobacco port on the Ohio River. Dover would be their point of departure. About a mile and a half east, across the river in Ripley, Ohio, the Reverend John Rankin, a Presbyterian minister, and his wife, Jean, would receive the girl and help move her on to the next station.

The Rankins' house sat far above the Ohio River, visible in an open clearing of trees with a lantern shining brightly in a window for all to see. All Arnold had to do was row the girl across the river, look for the house with the light, and listen for a bell tinkling in the air. He was assured that the Rankins had people on the bank of the river waiting to direct fugitive slaves up the hill to safety.

The next evening Arnold Gragston found himself back at the old woman's house, with the big-eyed, beautiful girl staring at him. The two teenagers made their way down the steep bank of the river, climbing into a waiting skiff and pushing away from the shore. Arnold glanced nervously around. Even a direct line across the Ohio River seemed a great distance. As he rowed in the stiff current, the night was so dark that their progress was hard to determine, and the minutes felt like hours. At last Arnold saw a light high on the hill, beckoning to them like a lighthouse guiding sailors to shore.

Arnold slid the skiff silently ashore. At that moment two men appeared and grabbed the girl, pulling her from the boat. Arnold trembled with fear and began to pray. Someone grabbed his own arm and said, "You hungry, boy?" The last thing he had expected was being offered something to eat.

The girl was in good hands now. Arnold turned around and rowed himself back to Kentucky, hoping he would make it home undetected. The pretty girl was gone forever. She was well on her way to freedom, and Arnold was headed home with plenty to think about. Arnold would later recall: "I don't know how I ever rowed the boat across the river. The current was strong and I was trembling. I couldn't see a thing there in the dark, but I felt that girl's eyes. We didn't dare to whisper. So I couldn't tell her how sure I was that Mr. Tabb or some of the other owners would 'tear me up' when they found out what I had done. I just knew they would find out."

Although it took a while for Arnold to recover from his terrifying first trip across the river, he eventually realized that he could do it again. It came to be a well-kept secret that he was willing to assist runaways across the river. Typically, he preferred to meet his passengers on the darkest nights when their features would be obscured and he would thus later have a hard time identifying them. As the forms came up to him, Arnold would whisper, "What you say?" and if the correct password was given—"menare"—he would take them across the river. Arnold never knew the word's meaning but thought it might have been a biblical term, though no such word is known.

Arnold Gragston began making three or four trips a month across the Ohio River, rowing under the night skies. Sometimes he carried just a few people; other times his skiff was full. Sometimes Arnold risked hiding fugitive slaves in barns until the "black nights" of the moon arrived. Instead of gaining his own freedom, he helped others attain theirs. Over a four-year period from 1859 to 1863, he helped liberate close to three hundred slaves, and never did he ask for anything in return.

In 1863 after rowing twelve fugitives across the river, Arnold was nearly apprehended. To avoid being caught, he hid out for weeks, sleeping in fields and in the woods. His days of portaging passengers to freedom were over. He was married by this time, and when an opportunity finally presented itself, he took his wife Sallie as his last passenger across the Ohio River. It seemed like he was pulling the weight of the world in the boat that night, rowing them toward the familiar light up the bank.

Arnold and Sallie Gragston went on to Detroit, Michigan, for fear of being captured, coming back to Bracken County, Kentucky, to farm in the 1880s. They would have ten children and thirty-one grandchildren. Over the years Arnold would visit his family who lived on land that had once been the Tabb farm where Gragston had been enslaved. He would sit on the front porch, in a chair surrounded by his great-great-grandchildren, and retell the story of his first adventure across the Ohio River. Upon his death in 1938, well into his nineties, Arnold was fondly remembered as a wonderful storyteller. He would recount river crossings during storms, using leaky boats, and sometimes having to threaten passengers to silence so as not to alert the patrollers.

The Broadway Christian Church in Germantown, Kentucky, where Arnold Gragston was both a deacon and cofounder, still holds monthly services to this day. A historic marker in Germantown reminds everyone that Arnold Gragston's story was one of courage and hope. This well-respected, daring oarsman was laid to rest in the Greenlawn Cemetery in Ripley, Ohio, where he had first rowed so many to freedom.

WHAT GOES AROUND COMES AROUND
Mattie Jane Jackson's Revenge

1864

Just as Mattie Jane Jackson was walking up the plank to the ferry that would lead her to freedom, she felt the cord around her waist loosen. The bundle of clothes hidden beneath her hoop skirt had begun to slide slowly to the ground. Mattie tripped slightly over the tangle at her ankles, but tried to act as if nothing was wrong.

Mattie J. Jackson was born into slavery in 1846 in Saint Louis, Missouri. Mattie's mother and siblings had tried to escape numerous times over the years on their own, but had always failed. Over time Mattie realized she would probably need assistance from others to be successful.

By age eighteen, Mattie was determined to have her freedom at last. Mattie's current master and mistress, Captain and Mrs. Ephraim Frisbee, were much improved over any earlier owners, and fortunately she was given certain privileges.

Mattie knew her best opportunity to escape would be during one of those occasions twice a month when she was allowed away for two hours to go to church. These excursions became fact-finding missions, and after several inquiries Mattie had learned of some black folks who helped fugitive slaves. A plan was concocted, and Mattie was told that she had to adhere strictly to the schedule. Things had to run like clockwork if they were to succeed.

The escape plan was six months in the making. When the day finally came in September 1864, however, everything seemed to go wrong. On a Sunday evening Mattie asked permission to attend church service, to which her mistress reluctantly agreed. It seemed Mistress Frisbee sensed Mattie's eagerness and deliberately found additional tasks for Mattie to complete to her satisfaction before leaving. Master Frisbee then joined in with his own requests, purposely delaying her departure.

At long last Mattie retired to her quarters and set the plan into action. She had to take her clothes with her, as it would be impossible to replace her meager wardrobe. She tied nine articles of clothing, which was all she owned, into tidy bundles and attached them to a thin cord tied around her waist. Mattie made sure the cumbersome bundle hidden underneath her dress did not distort the evenness of the circular hoops of her skirt. She practiced walking around the small room thus attired. The weighted bundle intensified the pain her side gave her at the least exertion.

Just as Mattie was finally ready to leave, she was called upon to dress the Frisbees' young son for a family carriage ride. As she attended to the boy under the watchful eyes of Mistress Frisbee, Mattie backed into a corner, putting the boy between her and the woman. When exiting the room, Mattie was acutely aware of the clothes dangling under her dress, and of the thin cord that supported them biting into her waist. She attempted to maneuver out of the room without an affected gait.

Later, as Mattie was walking on the road to church, the Frisbee family's carriage sped past her in a cloud of dust. Mattie picked up her pace. She had taken $25 of her master's money, which she needed to cover travel expenses. Mattie wanted to be long gone before the theft was discovered.

Coming into town, Mattie saw a man on the opposite side of the street who appeared to be waiting for no one in particular. As she drew near, the gentleman turned and walked ahead. As planned, Mattie followed him at a safe distance. As they approached the church, the man dropped off to the side. Mattie stayed and waited for her next connection. Twilight began to spread over the small Missouri town. She soon noticed two young ladies chatting quietly. When Mattie walked up to them, one discreetly slipped a pass into Mattie's hand and told her to follow along behind, leaving a block's distance between them.

The ladies led her to the river, where a ferry awaited. Mattie fell in line behind a group of Union soldiers about to board the ferry, trying to look as if she was accustomed to traveling on a boat. She presented her pass with an air of confidence, though she could not hear a thing above the beating of her heart. The ticket agent simply nodded her on. The plan seemed to be progressing without a hitch.

It was then that Mattie felt the rope cutting into her waist give way. Feeling the clothes slip from position, Mattie tried not to panic. The last thing she wanted was to draw attention to herself. Some soldiers nearby noticed her slight stumble but then turned away again, lost in conversation. With the bundle of clothes now at her feet, Mattie stooped slightly, maneuvering her hoop skirt in such a way as to allow her to push the bundle along concealing it with her feet, first one foot then the other, in slow, steady movements. If the bundle revealed itself, she would be exposed as a fugitive slave. Finally she found a seat out of the way, and calmly sat down as if nothing out of the ordinary had happened. When no one else was near, she reattached the cord holding the bundle.

Mattie floated away on her ferry, leaving behind eighteen years of bondage. She later boarded the railcars waiting in Jefferson City that would take her to freedom in Indianapolis, Indiana.

Along the journey Mattie remembered how her father had escaped to Chicago when she was three years old. And how two years later her mother, Ellen Turner, followed with Mattie and her sister, but they were gone just two days before being apprehended in Illinois. Then came a week in prison and four weeks in Linch's slave trader's yard until they were all sold to the cruel William Lewis. During her enslavement Mattie's mother had married twice. Both husbands, Westley Jackson and George Brown, had managed to escape, but neither was able to secure freedom for her or the children they had fathered.

Mattie Jane Jackson thought about all her masters and mistresses while enslaved. Mr. and Mrs. Lewis had proven to be the worst owners Mattie and her family had ever had. They were impossible to please, and their irrational anger resulted in beatings with both fists and whips. Mattie recalled how the Lewises sold Mattie and her mother, sister, and half brother to Captain Tirrell, who attempted to smuggle them out of the state before President Lincoln's Emancipation Proclamation of 1863 rendered them valueless. Over the years they had been sold, kidnapped, and resold many times. They had endured hateful masters and vindictive mistresses.

Mattie was understandably overjoyed when she arrived in Indianapolis, Indiana. She soon began work as a servant, finding it surreal to be actually paid for working. It would be three months until her mother dared run away.

In May 1864 Mattie's younger sister, Esther, escaped to free soil, but they were never reunited. Later that summer Mattie's mother's seventh escape attempt succeeded. She and Mattie's younger half brother, George, found their way to Mattie in Indianapolis for a heartfelt reunion.

The three immediately returned to their native city of Saint Louis, Missouri. After the war Mattie's mother married her third husband, Sam Adams. Her first husband, Westley Jackson, lived as a free man in Chicago, but died before the war. Her second husband, George Brown, had changed his name to John G. Thompson when he took refuge in Canada. He remarried after hearing that his family had died in an escape attempt.

In 1866 George Brown (John G. Thompson) learned that his son, George, and stepdaughter, Mattie, were still alive. He and his wife, Dr. L. S. Thompson, made arrangements for them to come to Lawrence, Massachusetts, for a reunion. Mattie's stepmother, Dr. Thompson, was a botanical physician, an abolitionist, and a worker on the Underground Railroad. She helped Mattie publish her life story in 1866 in an attempt to secure funds for Mattie's education.

In 1869 twenty-three-year-old Mattie Jane Jackson married a Mississippi steamboat porter, William Reed Dyer. They had eight children, four of whom lived to adulthood. Mattie lived to the age of sixty-three in and around her birthplace of Saint Louis as a free woman. She recalled how she once found a moment of sweet revenge for her years of enslavement.

Upon her return to Saint Louis, she experienced a strange twist of fate after the Civil War ended slavery. Mattie and her mother came across their former master and mistress, the cruel Lewises, on the streets of Saint Louis. Mr. and Mrs. Lewis had been so severe and abusive that they had often beaten them both at the slightest provocation. Mattie's mother recognized Mrs. Lewis at the market; Mrs. Lewis and her children were in a much-reduced and humbled station, being now forced to "wait upon themselves." Mr. Lewis was quite astonished to see Mattie as a free woman and inadvertently dropped her a bow before realizing he had just shown respect to his former slave. The only thing Mattie then had to conceal was a smile.

ON A DARE
John Parker's Double Life

Mid-1860s

It was well after midnight when John Parker crept up to the back of a slave owner's house in Kentucky and slipped through the kitchen door. As his eyes adjusted to the gloom, he saw the light of a candle shining out from underneath a bedroom door. He cocked his head to listen for snoring. It seemed like a simple enough mission. All he needed to do was sneak undetected into that bedroom, steal an infant, and then find a way to make his exit without being detected and shot. Mindful of the squeaky floorboards, he took another carefully placed step into the room. Such rescue attempts assuaged Parker's rage at once being enslaved himself.

John P. Parker had grown up an angry child. At eight years old, having just been separated from his mother and forced to walk from Norfolk, Virginia, to Richmond in a chain gang of slaves, his anger was directed at anything in nature that, unlike him, was free. After Richmond he was sold to a slave trader and suffered the indignity of being shackled to others in a four-hundred-slave caravan on a grueling eight-hundred-mile march to Alabama.

When John was sold, he worked as a house servant for an Alabama doctor, whose sons taught him to read. As he grew older, John Parker became a determined, hardworking, intelligent young man. He was apprenticed at a foundry and mastered iron molding. Having been unsuccessful at escaping, Parker convinced a new owner to let him work out his freedom. After a two-year period, he saved the requisite $1,800 and became free at age eighteen. In 1848 he married and settled in Ripley, Ohio, a bustling river port fifty miles east of Cincinnati. Parker could look out over the north bank of the Ohio River to the slave state of Kentucky from his front yard.

John Parker owned his home on 300 Front Street. He and his partner opened an iron foundry and blacksmith shop in Ripley, where he employed both black and white workers. He was seen as a well-regarded, upstanding citizen. During the day Parker ran his business. At night, however, he became a slave runner. Many evenings while his family slept, Parker would walk out his front door and pursue his clandestine work as an agent and conductor on the Underground Railroad.

When confronted, Parker adamantly denied aiding fugitive slaves: Such foolishness would put him and his family at risk. During one of his many forays into Kentucky, however, he noticed a poster with a thousand-dollar reward for his capture, dead or alive. Apparently regional slave catchers had their suspicions. Parker refused to be intimidated. Though of large stature, he armed himself and acquired the habit of walking down the middle of the street, day or night, so that he would not be abducted into an alley. Fear of being kidnapped was a harsh reality for free blacks—especially so for Parker, with a price on his head.

In the mid-1860s a white employee at Parker's foundry, Jim
Shroufe, baited him, challenging that if Parker was so brazen, he
should prove it by stealing some of Shroufe's father's slaves in Kentucky. Jim Shroufe was a paid patroller one mile east of Dover, just
one and a half miles west of Ripley. Parker outwardly ignored the
man, but secretly took the dare.

That very night, John Parker rowed quietly across the Ohio River
to Shroufe's Kentucky home directly across from the west end of Ripley. He tied off his boat and stealthily made his way up the steep, tree-
lined bank below Shroufe's house. This first attempt, however, wasn't
meant to be. In the darkness, following a form down a dirt road, he
soon saw that he was mistakenly following a white man. He feared
that it might be one of Shroufe's other sons, John, who was a slave
patroller east of Dover, Kentucky, and not someone Parker wanted to
run into. Parker narrowly escaped this unwanted encounter and, for
the moment, aborted the rescue mission.

Three nights later, Parker was able to identify himself to one of
Shroufe's slaves and reveal his plans. The man wanted to escape but
explained he had a small family and could not leave without his wife
and baby. Parker knew from experience that babies were especially
problematic but agreed to take them all the following week. Just as
they were finalizing their plans, however, a slave patroller appeared
out of nowhere and attacked Parker with a club. Parker threw dirt
in his assailant's eyes and made a run for the river, rowing home
while the slave took off for his cabin. The following day at work, Jim
Shroufe did not seem to have any knowledge of the incident.

The following week, John Parker rowed across the river in the
dark of night, silently dipping his oars, propelling himself closer to
possibly losing his own freedom. He hid the boat from the prying
eyes of the patrollers and took off to find the young family.

Parker soon learned that Mr. Shroufe had been growing suspicious of his slaves' actions. Shroufe and his wife were keeping the couple's baby in their own bedroom at night to prevent the slave family from running away. A gun and a candle were on a chair next to their bed.

The slave mother and father told Parker about the problem and insisted they would not leave without their baby. The only solution was for Parker to sneak into the Shroufes' bedroom and snatch the baby right out from under their noses. The slave mother, who worked in the main house, described the layout of the L-shaped, two-story brick home. Parker instructed the nervous parents to be ready to flee as soon as he returned with their baby. He removed his shoes so he could move quietly about the house and gave them to the man for safekeeping.

As Parker entered through the kitchen door at the back of the house, he saw two rooms. He let his eyes adjust to the sliver of candle-light coming from the bedroom and eased barefoot across the rough plank floorboards. Carefully, he tried the latch on the bedroom door. On his third attempt, the door creaked slowly open. It sounded very loud, but the heavy breathing inside assured him that the Shroufes were fast asleep. After surveying the room, Parker noticed that Mr. Shroufe was lying nearest the door. The candle on the chair illuminated not one but two pistols.

Parker surmised that the baby was on the woman's side of the bed. As he lowered himself to the floor and crawled forward, the bedroom door swung shut behind him. Undaunted, he reached up for the bundle on the bed, pulling what he hoped was the baby toward him. The bed creaked loudly. Parker felt sure he had been discovered. He grabbed the baby and bolted for the door.

A chair crashed to the floor behind him, extinguishing the candle. The startled Mr. Shroufe felt around in the darkness for his weapons. Parker raced out the kitchen door, clutching the child. Together with the baby's parents, he ran toward the river. As they ran past the slave quarters, the parents yelled that they needed to go back to their log cabin for something. Parker kept running, calling back that if they wanted to see the baby again, they had better follow him.

The couple ran after him down to the Ohio River—a distance of about a thousand feet. There was another boat at the landing, and they pushed it adrift so that it could not be used in a chase. They scrambled into Parker's skiff as he began rowing earnestly across the Ohio River in the dark. Shroufe's voice could be heard from the dock angrily calling after them as bullets whined over their heads.

John Parker rowed upriver instead of directly across to his house. When they landed, Parker asked for his shoes. Unbelievably, the man claimed not to have had time to go back and get them. An infuriated Parker knew that his shoes could identify him. If convicted of assisting with a slave escape, he could have all his possessions confiscated and receive a prison sentence of up to twenty years. However, he had time only to concentrate on the task at hand, which was to make this newly rescued family disappear.

Parker took the fugitives to an abolitionist lawyer friend who would forward them on. With that done, Parker then ran to his house, undressed, jumped into bed, and waited.

Before he'd hardly had time to catch his breath, there was a pounding at his front door and angry voices demanding to see him. Parker came to the bedroom window in his nightshirt, seemingly irritated to have been awoken. Jim Shroufe was surprised to see Parker at home. Still he accused him of stealing his father's slaves, including the baby. Parker acted like Shroufe was out of his mind and purposely took his time getting dressed. He did not usually allow slave hunters to search his home, but this time he needed to give the fugitives a head start. After an exhaustive search, Jim Shroufe and his father, pistols in hand, were sorely disappointed not to find their slaves.

The next day a triumphant Jim Shroufe showed up at work carrying Parker's shoes. Parker, fortunate to have another pair of shoes, claimed never to have seen them before. Shroufe went to every shoe merchant in town, hoping to snare Parker, but no one gave Parker up. The defeated, disgruntled employee never came back to work at Parker's iron foundry again. He knew as well as Parker did that the man, woman, and baby were well into their 250-mile journey to Canada.

John P. Parker and his wife, Miranda, had six children. Within two generations the Parkers went from being enslaved to being college educated. Parker owned a foundry, a blacksmith shop, and a machine shop, and was one of few black men before 1900 to receive patents for his inventions (including a portable screw tobacco press and a clod-smashing machine). For nearly fifteen years he had courageously put his life on the line in the name of freedom, successfully bringing at least one thousand men, women, and children to freedom's shore. It was his way of dealing with his "eternal hatred of the institution" of slavery. The angry little boy had grown into a man who devoted his life to liberating the oppressed and preventing the strong from destroying the weak.

Upon John Parker's death in 1900, the *Cincinnati Commercial Tribune* wrote this tribute to the Ripley, Ohio, man who ran a successful business by day and operated as a conductor on the Underground Railroad at night: "A more fearless creature never lived. He gloried in danger. . . . He would go boldly over into the enemy's camp and filch the fugitives to freedom."

UNDERGROUND RAILROAD FACTS AND TRIVIA

- More than four million slaves were set free when the Civil War ended in 1865.
- It is estimated that from forty thousand to one hundred thousand slaves escaped bondage, with a large portion going through the state of Ohio on their way to Canada.
- William Still, a free black man in Pennsylvania, was known as the "Father of the Underground Railroad."
- Most Underground Railroad station houses did not have secret rooms and spaces but used existing hiding spaces such as attics, barns, cellars, or closets.
- Spirituals such as "When I'm Gone" and "Wade in the Water, Children" were used as codes to inform others about slaves escaping.
- Levi Coffin, a white Quaker in Indiana, was known as the "President of the Underground Railroad."
- It was common practice for slave families to be part slave, part free, as they purchased their freedom one member at a time.
- A slave caught by a patroller without a pass could be whipped.
- Plantation owners provided food and shelter for slaves with passes on errands from other plantations.
- Gangs of kidnappers, especially in the mid-Atlantic states, made money by kidnapping free blacks and selling them into slavery.
- Twelve American presidents owned slaves, and eight of them owned slaves while serving as president.

- The transatlantic slave trade was abolished in 1808 when the United States made importing slaves from Africa a federal crime, but smuggling continued until the Civil War.
- Slave families were divided when the master of a plantation died and his estate (including his slave property) was divided up among his heirs. Slaves were used to obtain credit and pay off debts.
- The Fugitive Slave Act of 1850 allowed runaway slaves to be pursued out of state and returned to slavery if ownership could be established. The law made aiding fugitives a criminal offense, but states varied in their punishment. A conviction could carry a penalty of six months in jail, a $1,000 fine, and a civil liability of $1,000 for each fugitive. Such convictions damaged a person's reputation and social standing in the community.
- Slaves who could not tolerate their living conditions sometimes went on strike or were "lying out." They temporarily ran away, and word was sent to their masters that unless a certain condition was met, they would run away permanently.
- Philadelphia, Pennsylvania, boasted the nation's first formally organized antislavery society.
- According to Wilbur H. Siebert, a foremost authority, there were more than 3,200 documented people who worked on the Underground Railroad. Countless others remain unnamed.
- Canada became a refuge for escaping slaves after the passage of antislavery legislation on July 9, 1793. During the War of 1812, thousands of blacks who volunteered to fight with the British were promised their freedom and land in Canada, creating an even greater incentive for blacks to move there.
- The American Anti-slavery Society, with both black and white members, was formed in 1833 to heighten awareness of the injustices of slavery and to support its abolition. Within five years it had a quarter million members.

- By law the children followed the status of their mother. If she was free, they were born free; if she was a slave, they were born slaves.
- In 1777 Vermont became the first state to abolish slavery.
- Calvin Fairbank was arrested twice for taking fugitive slaves over the Ohio River to freedom. He was given a fifteen-year sentence, the longest given to an Underground Railroad activist.
- In 1859, 16 percent of the total United States population was black.
- The most heavily traveled route along the Underground Railroad went through Ohio, Indiana, and western Pennsylvania.
- Slavery was abolished in the British Empire, including Canada, in 1833.
- The American Colonization Society, founded in 1816, established the colony of Liberia, where freed slaves were removed to settle their own community on the west coast of Africa.
- Warring African tribes sold their captives to European ship owners. In 1619 the Dutch sold slaves to settlers in Jamestown, the first permanent English settlement in North America.
- Slavery existed in America from the earliest period of colonial settlement at the beginning of the seventeenth century until it was abolished in 1865 by passage of the Thirteenth Amendment.
- Ohio was a center of high activity on the Underground Railroad because it bordered the slave states of Kentucky and Virginia, and it was linked to Canada by Lake Erie.
- After the passage of the Fugitive Slave Act of 1850, many blacks fled to Canada. Not all of them returned to the United States after slavery was abolished in 1865.
- Serious scholars refute the claim that patterned quilts had encoded messages that showed slaves the way to freedom. Some of the quilt patterns originated much later in the 1930s.

- President Lincoln's Emancipation Proclamation on January 1, 1863, altered how black people in the South celebrated New Year's Day. Previously the day was known as "Heartbreak Day," a day when families were torn apart through sales at auctions or individuals left to be hired out on other plantations.
- The National Underground Railroad Network to Freedom in Omaha, Nebraska, in association with the National Park Service (NPS), lists sites that have approved documentation in connection with the Underground Railroad. There are currently 552 listings—380 sites, 107 programs, and 65 facilities—in 36 states and the District of Columbia.

BIBLIOGRAPHY

BOOKS

Abajian, James de T., comp. *Blacks in Selected Newspapers, Censuses and Other Sources: An Index to Names and Subjects.* Vols. 1, 2, 3. Boston: G. K. Hall & Company, 1977.

Anderson, Jean Bradley. *Piedmont Plantation: The Bennehan-Cameron Family and Lands in North Carolina.* Durham: University of North Carolina Publisher Association, 2000.

Andrews, William L., ed. *Narrative of the Life of Frederick Douglass, an American Slave, Written by Himself.* New York: W. W. Norton & Company, 1997.

———. Introduction to *Six Women's Slave Narratives.* New York: Oxford University Press, 1988.

Baker, Roger. *Clara: An Ex-Slave in Gold Rush Colorado.* Central City, CO: Black Hawk Publishing, 2003.

Berlin, Ira. *Generations of Captivity: A History of African-American Slaves.* Cambridge, MA: Belknap Press of Harvard University Press, 2003.

Berlin, Ira, Marc Favreau, and Steven F. Miller, eds. *Remembering Slavery: African Americans Talk about Their Personal Experiences of Slavery and Freedom.* New York: New Press, 1998.

Blassingame, John, ed. *Slave Testimonies: Two Centuries of Letters, Speeches, Interviews, and Autobiographies.* Baton Rouge: Louisiana State University Press, 1977.

Blight, David W., ed. *Passages to Freedom: The Underground Railroad in History and Memory.* Washington, DC: Smithsonian Books, 2004.

Blockson, Charles L. *Hippocrene Guide to the Underground Railroad.* New York: Hippocrene Books, 1994.

———. *The Underground Railroad: Dramatic Firsthand Accounts of Daring Escapes to Freedom.* New York: Berkeley Books, 1987.

Bolden, Tonya. *The Book of African-American Women: 150 Crusaders, Creators, and Uplifters.* Holbrook, MA: Adams Media, 1996.

Bontemps, Arna. Introduction to *Five Black Lives: The Autobiographies of Venture Smith, James Mars, William Grimes, the Reverend G. W. Offley, and James L. Smith.* 1855. Reprint, Middleton, CT: Wesleyan University Press, 1971.

———. *Great Slave Narratives.* Boston: Beacon Press, 1969.

Bordewich, Fergus M. *Bound for Canaan: The Underground Railroad and the War for the Soul of America.* New York: Amistad, 2005.

Botkin, Benjamin Albert. *Lay My Burden Down: A Folk History of Slavery.* Chicago: University of Chicago Press, 1945.

Brown, John. *Slave Life in Georgia: A Narrative of the Life, Sufferings, and Escape of John Brown, a Fugitive Slave.* Savannah, GA: Beehive Press, 1855.

Carbone, Elisa Lynn. *Stealing Freedom.* New York: Random House, 1999.

Cecelski, David S. *The Waterman's Song: Slavery and Freedom in Maritime North Carolina.* Chapel Hill: University of North Carolina Press, 2001.

Century, Douglas. *Toni Morrison.* New York: Chelsea House Publishers, 1994.

Chase, Henry. *In Their Footsteps: The American Visions Guide to African-American Heritage Sites.* New York: Henry Holt, 1948.

Coffin, Levi. *Reminiscences of Levi Coffin, the Reputed President of the Underground Railroad; Being a Brief History of the Labors of a Lifetime in Behalf of the Slave, with the Stories of Numerous Fugitives, Who Gained Their Freedom through His Instrumentality, and Many Other Incidents.* Cincinnati, OH: Western Tract Society, 1876.

Cohen, Anthony. *The Underground Railroad in Montgomery County, Maryland: A History and Driving Guide.* Rockville, MD: Montgomery County Historical Society, 1995.

Craft, William, and Ellen Craft. *Running a Thousand Miles for Freedom: The Escape of William and Ellen Craft from Slavery.* Athens: University of Georgia Press, 1999. First published 1860 by Brown Thrasher Books, London.

Danforth, Mildred E. *A Quaker Pioneer: Laura Haviland, Superintendent of the Underground.* New York: Exposition Press, 1961.

DeRamus, Betty. *Forbidden Fruit: Love Stories from the Underground Railroad.* New York: Atria Books, 2005.

Douglass, Frederick. *Narrative of the Life of Frederick Douglass, an American Slave, Written by Himself.* New York: New American Library, 1968. First published 1845 by Boston Antislavery Society.

Drayton, Daniel. *Personal Memoir of Daniel Drayton, for Four Years and Four Months a Prisoner (for Charity's Sake) in Washington Jail, Including a Narrative of the Voyage and the Capture of the Schooner Pearl.* 1855. Reprint, New York: Negro Universities Press, 1969.

Dykstra, Robert R. *Bright Radical Star: Black Freedom and White Supremacy on the Hawkeye Frontier.* Ames: Iowa State University Press, 1997.

Eakin, Sue. *Solomon Northup's Twelve Years a Slave: 1841–1853.* Gretna, LA: Pelican Publishing, 1998.

Ex-Slave Narratives. Brooksville, KY: Bracken County Historical Society, 2001.

Fiske, David, Clifford W. Brown, and Rachel Seligman. *Solomon Northup: The Complete Story of the Author of "Twelve Years a Slave."* Santa Barbara, CA: Praeger, 2013.

Fleischner, Jennifer. *I Was Born a Slave: The Story of Harriet Jacobs.* Brookfield, CT: Millbrook Press, 1997.

Foner, Philip S. *History of Black Americans from the Compromise of 1850 to the End of the Civil War.* Westport, CT: Greenwood Press, 1983.

———. *History of Black Americans from the Emergence of the Cotton Kingdom to the Eve of the Compromise of 1850.* Westport, CT: Greenwood Press, 1983.

Fradin, Dennis Brindell. *Bound for the North Star: True Stories of Fugitive Slaves.* New York: Clarion Books, 2000.

Franklin, John Hope, and Alfred A. Moss, Jr. *From Slavery to Freedom.* New York: McGraw-Hill, 2000.

Franklin, John Hope, and Loren Schweninger. *Runaway Slaves: Rebels on the Plantation.* New York: Oxford University Press, 2000.

Gaines, Edith M. *Freedom Light: Underground Railroad Stories from Ripley, Ohio.* Cleveland, OH: New Day Press, 1991.

Gates, Henry Louis, Jr. Foreword to *Unchained Memories: Readings from the Slave Narratives.* Boston: Bulfinch Press, 2002.

Goodall, Hurley C., comp. *Underground Railroad: The Invisible Road to Freedom through Indiana.* Indiana: Works Progress Administration Writers Project, 2000.

Grover, Kathryn. *The Fugitive's Gibraltar: Escaping Slaves and Abolitionism in New Bedford, Massachusetts.* Amherst: University of Massachusetts Press, 2001.

Gutman, Herbert. *The Black Family in Slavery and Freedom, 1750–1925.* New York: Pantheon Books, Vintage, 1976.

Hagedorn, Ann. *Beyond the River: The Untold Story of the Heroes of the Underground Railroad.* New York: Simon & Schuster, 2002.

Hamilton, Virginia. *The People Could Fly: American Black Folktales.* New York: Knopf, 1985.

Harris, Middleton, comp. *The Black Book.* With the assistance of Morris Levitt, Roger Furman, and Ernest Smith. New York: Random House, 1974.

Haviland, Laura S. *A Woman's Work: Labors and Experiences of Laura S. Haviland 1808–1898.* Cincinnati, OH: Walden & Stowe, 1882.

Helper, Hinton Rowan. *The Impending Crisis of the South.* New York: A. B. Burdick, 1857.

Hendrick, George and Willene. *Fleeing for Freedom: Stories of the Underground Railroad.* Chicago: Ivan R. Dee, 2004.

Hilty, Hiram H. *By Land and by Sea: Quakers Confront Slavery and Its Aftermath in North Carolina.* Greensboro: North Carolina Friends Historical Society, 1993.

Hoobler, Dorothy, and Thomas Hoobler. *The African American Family Album.* New York: Oxford City Press, 1995.

Horton, James Oliver, and Lois E. Horton. *Slavery and the Making of America.* Oxford: Oxford University Press, 2005.

Hurmence, Belinda, ed. *Forty-Eight Oral Histories of Former North and South Carolina Slaves.* New York: Penguin Books, 1990.

Jacobs, Harriet Ann. *Incidents in the Life of a Slave Girl. Written by Herself.* Boston: Published for the author, 1861.

Jones, Friday. *Days of Bondage: Autobiography of Friday Jones, Being a Brief Narrative of His Trials and Tribulations in Slavery.* Washington, DC: Commercial Publishing Co., 1883.

Kallen, Stuart A. *The Way People Live: Life on the Underground Railroad.* San Diego: Lucent Books, 2000.

Landau, Elaine. *Slave Narratives: The Journey to Freedom.* New York: Franklin Watts, 2001.

Lowery, Linda. *One More Valley, One More Hill: The Story of Aunt Clara Brown.* New York: Random House, 2002.

Lucas, Marion Brunson. *A History of Blacks in Kentucky from Slavery to Segregation, 1760–1891.* Frankfort: Kentucky Historical Society, 2003.

Lyons, Mary E. *Letters from a Slave Girl: The Story of Harriet Jacobs.* New York: Simon Pulse, 1992.

Maruyama, Susan J. *Perseverance: African Americans, Voices of Triumph.* Alexandria, VA: Time-Life Books, 1993.

McDougall, Marion Gleason. *Fugitive Slaves 1619–1865.* New York: Bergman Publishers, 1969.

Mellon, James, ed. *Bullwhip Days: The Slaves Remember; An Oral History.* New York: Avon Books, 1990.

Miller, Randall M. *"Dear Master": Letters of a Slave Family.* Ithaca, NY: Cornell University Press, 1978.

Miller, Ruth. *Black American Literature, 1760–Present.* New York: Macmillan, 1971.

Nathans, Sydney. *To Free a Family: The Journey of Mary Walker.* Cambridge, MA: Harvard University Press, 2012.

Nichols, Charles H. *Black Men in Chains.* New York: Lawrence Hill Co., 1972.

———. *Many Thousand Gone: The Ex-Slaves' Account of Their Bondage and Freedom.* Leiden, Germany: E. J. Brill, 1963.

Nine, Darlene Clark. *Black Women in American History from Colonial Times through the Nineteenth Century.* Brooklyn, NY: Carlson Publishing, 1990.

Northup, Solomon. *Twelve Years a Slave.* Mineola, NY: Dover Publications, 2014.

Paynter, John H. *Fugitives of Daniel Drayton.* New York: AMS Press, 1930.

Perdue, Charles L., Jr., Thomas E. Barden, and Robert K. Phillips, eds. *Weevils in the Wheat.* Charlottesville: University Press of Virginia, 1976.

Pickard, Kate. *The Kidnapped and the Ransomed.* New York: Negro University Press, 1968.

Rankin, Reverend John. *Letters on American Slavery Addressed to Mr. Thomas Rankin, Merchant at Middlebrook, Augusta County, Virginia.* Boston: Garrison & Knapp, 1833; and Isaac Knapp, 5th ed., 1839.

Rappaport, Doreen. *Freedom River.* New York: Jump at the Sun Hyperion Books for Children, 2000.

Rawick, George P., ed. *The American Slave: A Composite Autobiography.* Federal Writers' Project. Westport, CT: Greenwood Publishing Co., 1972.

Robertson, Stacey M. *Hearts Beating for Liberty: Women Abolitionists in the Old Northwest.* Chapel Hill: University of North Carolina Press, 2010.

Schlissel, Lillian. *Black Frontiers: A History of African-American Heroes in the Old West.* New York: Simon & Schuster Books for Young Readers, 1995.

Schneider, Dorothy, and Carl J. Schneider. *An Eyewitness History of Slavery in America from Colonial Times to the Civil War.* New York: Checkmark Books, 2000.

Seibert, Wilbur Henry. *The Underground Railroad from Slavery to Freedom.* New York: Russell & Russell, 1967.

Silag, Bill, ed. *Outside In: African-American History in Iowa 1838–2000.* Des Moines: State Historical Society of Iowa, 2001.

Smedley, Robert C. *History of the Underground Railroad in Chester and the Neighboring Counties of Pennsylvania.* 1883. Reprint, New York: Negro Universities Press, 1968.

Smith, James L. *Autobiography of James L. Smith, Including, Also, Reminiscences of Slave Life, Recollections of the War, Education of Freedmen, Causes of the Exodus, Etc.* Miami, FL: Mnemosyne Publishing Co., 1969. First published 1881 by Press of the Bulletin Company, Norwich, CT.

———. *Recollections of a Former Slave.* New York: Humanity Books, 2004.

Smith, Jessie Carney, ed. *Epic Lives: One Hundred Black Women Who Made a Difference.* Detroit, MI: Visible Ink Press, 1993.

Sprague, Stuart Seely, ed. *The Autobiography of John P. Parker, His Promised Land.* New York: W. W. Norton & Company, 1996.

Steele, James. *Freedom's River: The African-American Contribution to Democracy.* Chicago: Franklin Watts, 1994.

Sterling, Dorothy, ed. *We Are Your Sisters: Black Women in the Nineteenth Century.* New York: W. W. Norton & Company, 1984.

Still, William. *The Underground Railroad.* Chicago: Johnson Publishing Company, 1970.

Stowe, Harriet Beecher. *A Key to Uncle Tom's Cabin: Presenting the Original Facts and Documents upon Which the Story Is Founded. Together with Corroborative Statements Verifying the Truth of the Work.* Boston: John P. Jewett & Co., 1853.

Strother, Horatio T. *The Underground Railroad in Connecticut.* Middleton, CT: Wesleyan University Press, 1962.

Stroyer, Jacob. *My Life in the South in Five Slave Narratives, a Compendium.* New York: Arno Press and the New York Times, 1968.

Switala, William J. *Underground Railroad in Delaware, Maryland, and West Virginia.* Mechanicsburg, PA: Stackpole Books, 2004.

Talmadge, Marian. *Barney Ford, Black Baron.* New York: Dodd, Mead & Company, 1973.

Thompson, Dr. L. S. *The Story of Mattie J. Jackson: Her Parentage, Experience of Eighteen Years in Slavery, Incidents during the War, Her Escape from Slavery; A True Story.* Lawrence, MA: Printed at Sentinel Office, 1866.

Troester, Rosalie Riegle, ed. *Historic Women of Michigan: A Sesquicentennial Celebration.* Lansing: Michigan Women's Studies Association, 1987.

Yellin, Jean Fagan. *Harriet Jacobs: A Life.* New York: Basic Civitas Books, 2004.

Yetman, Norman, R. *Life Under the "Peculiar Institution": Selections from the Slave Narrative Collection.* New York: Holt, Rinehart and Winston, 1970.

BROCHURES

Exploring a Common Past: Researching and Interpreting the Underground Railroad. US Department of the Interior, National Park Service, History Office, National Register, History, and Education, 1998.

Historic Ripley, Ohio Freedom's Landing Underground Railroad Tour. Brown County, Ohio, Department of Economic Development, 2004.

John P. Parker 1827–1900. Ripley, OH: John P. Parker Historical Society.

Mary "Polly" Johnson 1784–1871. New Bedford, MA: New Bedford Historical Society.

Rankin House: Home of Reverend John Rankin, Abolitionist Freedom's Hero. Ripley, OH: Ripley Heritage, 1970.

The Underground Railroad. New Bedford, MA: New Bedford Whaling National Historical Park, 2001.

BIBLIOGRAPHY

MAGAZINES

Bea, Lena S. "Mary Walker's Family Story." *The Harvard Crimson*, February 2012.

Beal, M. Gertrude. "The Underground Railroad in Guilford County." *The Southern Friend* 2, no. 1 (Spring 1980): 18–28.

Berrier, G. Galin. "The Slaves of Ruel Daggs." *The Iowa Griot*, Summer 2002, 6–7. Publication of the African American Historical Museum and Cultural Center of Iowa, Cedar Rapids.

Blockson, Charles L. "Escape from Slavery: The Underground Railroad." *National Geographic*, July 1984, 2–39.

Chase, Henry. "Plotting a Course for Freedom; Paul Jennings: White House Memoirist–Servant of President James Madison; Special Issue: The Untold Story of Blacks in the White House." *American Visions* 10, no. 1 (February–March 1995): 52–54.

Coon, Diane Perrine. "Great Escapes: The Underground Railroad." *Northern Kentucky Heritage* 9, no. 2 (Spring/Summer 2002): 2–12.

Garretson, Owen A. "The Underground Railroad in Iowa." *Iowa Journal of History and Politic,* July 1924, 91.

Hatcher, Susan Tucker. "North Carolina Quakers: Bona Fide Abolitionists." *The Southern Friend* 1, no. 2 (Autumn 1979): 81–96.

Paynter, John H. "The Fugitives of the Pearl." *Journal of Negro History* 1, no. 3 (July 1916): 243–64.

"The Underground Railroad Freedom Center." *Ebony*, November 2004, 46–49.

Williams-Meyers, A. J. "Some Notes on the Extent of New York City's Involvement in the Underground Railroad." *Afro-Americans in New York Life and History* 29, no. 2 (July 2005): 73.

Yellin, Jean Fagan. "Written by Herself: Harriet Jacobs' Slave Narrative." *American Literature* 53.3 (1981): 379–486.

NEWSPAPERS

Chrastina, Paul. "Disguised as a White Man, Slave Takes Her Husband North." *Old News* (Landisville, PA), 1860.

Libby, Sam. "Jail Hill's Rich History Is Reborn in Research." *New York Times,* March 28, 1999.

Ricks, Mary Kay. "Escape on the Pearl." *Washington Post,* August 12, 1998.

Robichaux, Mark. "What Really Became of Solomon Northup after His '12 Years a Slave'?" Speakeasy, *Wall Street Journal,* October 23, 2013.

"Slave-Hunters in Boston." *Old Liberator,* November 1, 1850. "Some Boy to Attend Tech." *New Bedford Sunday Standard,* December 15, 1918.

Yardley, Jonathan. "A Literate Slave Who Ran Away." *Washington Post,* March 11, 2012.

OTHER

African-American Records of Bracken County, Kentucky: 1797–1999. Compiled by Caroline Miller. Vol. 1. Brooksville, KY: Bracken County Historical Society, 2000.

American History Series: A Slave's Story: Running a Thousand Miles to Freedom. Columbus, OH: Learning Corporation of America, 1990. VHS.

Broadway Christian Church deed. Germantown, KY, 1880.

Found Voices: The Slave Narratives. Princeton, NJ: Films for the Humanities and Sciences, 1999. VHS.

Handy, Delores. "Mary Walker's Descendants Realize Their Rich Family History." 90.9 WBUR audio, 4:20. February, 28, 2012. www.wbur.org/2012/02/28/mary-walker-descendants.

Smart-Grosvenor, Vertamae. *Slave Voices—Things Past Telling.* Produced and distributed by DIVE AUDIO, Beverly Hills, CA, 1992. VHS.

Twelve Years a Slave. Directed by Steve McQueen. 2013; Los Angeles: 20th Century Fox Home Entertainment, 2014. DVD.

Yellin, Jean Fagan. "Harriet Jacobs." In *Dictionary of North Carolina Biography.* Edited by William S. Powell. 6 vols. Chapel Hill: University of North Carolina Press, 1979.

WEBSITES

"The African-American Mosaic: A Library of Congress Resource Guide for the Study of Black History & Culture." Accessed December 10, 2014. www.lcweb.loc.gov/exhibits/african/intro.html.

"Born in Slavery: Slave Narratives from the Federal Writers' Project, 1936–1938." Joint presentation of the Manuscript and Prints and Photographs Divisions of the Library of Congress. Accessed December 10, 2014. www.memory.loc.gov/ammem/snhtml/snhome.html.

"Chesapeake and Delaware Canal." By Scott M. Kozel. Pennways, Roads to the Future. Accessed December 10, 2014. www.pennways.com/CD_Canal.html.

"Documenting the American South." Academic Affairs Library, University of North Carolina at Chapel Hill. Accessed December 10, 2014. www.docsouth.unc.edu.

"Harriet Jacobs: Selected Writings and Correspondence." Yale University. Accessed December 10, 2014. www.yale.edu/glc/harriet/docs.htm.

"Lest We Forget: The Triumph over Slavery." Archives and Special Collections, Schomburg Center for Research in Black Culture,

New York Public Library, 2004. Accessed December 10, 2014. http://digital.nypl.org/lwf.

National Underground Railroad Freedom Center. Accessed December 10, 2014. www.freedomcenter.org.

National Underground Railroad Network to Freedom. Accessed December 10, 2014. www.nps.gov/ugrr.

"Pathways to Freedom: Maryland & the Underground Railroad." Maryland Public Television, 2002. Accessed December 10, 2014. http://pathways.thinkport.org.

Solomon Northup Day, Saratoga Springs Visitor Center. Accessed December 10, 2014. www.saratogaspringsvisitorcenter.com/about-the.../solomon-northup-day.

Solomon Northup Day—A Celebration of Freedom, Skidmore College. Accessed December 10, 2014. www.skidmore.edu/solomon-northup-day.

INTERVIEWS

Baloyan, Greg, interviewed by Tricia Martineau Wagner, May 30, 2006.

Baxter, Marla, interviewed by Tricia Martineau Wagner, December 9, 2005.

Coutant, Betty, interviewed by Tricia Martineau Wagner, April 10, 2006.

David, Lynn, interviewed by Tricia Martineau Wagner, December 9, 2005.

Edwards, Lee, interviewed by Tricia Martineau Wagner, April 25, 2006.

Gindy, Gaye E., interviewed by Tricia Martineau Wagner, May 22, 2006.

BIBLIOGRAPHY

Johnson, Reverend William, interviewed by Tricia Martineau Wagner, March 4, 2006.

Miller, Caroline, interviewed by Tricia Martineau Wagner, January 5, 2006, March 3, 2006.

Rice, Major Ronald, interviewed by Tricia Martineau Wagner, April 22, 2006.

Schmidt, Eva, interviewed by Tricia Martineau Wagner, April 26, 2006.

Still, Clarence Harrison Jr., interviewed by Tricia Martineau Wagner, February 26, 2006.

Williams, Brenda Rice, interviewed by Tricia Martineau Wagner, April 29, 2006.

INDEX

abduction, 23, 29–30, 70, 90, 91, 140, 145. *See also* Northup, Solomon
abolition, 145, 147
abolitionists, 68, 76, 77, 82–83; Haviland in territory of, 38–39; Tom on, 42, 43
actor, 48
ads for runaway slaves, 8–9, 85–86, 105
Adams, Sam, 137
Adams, William, 85–87
Adams Express Office, 82
Adirondack Mountains, 28
Adrian, Michigan, 36, 38–39
agent, 67–68. *See also* Burris, Samuel D.; Parker, John
Alabama, 64, 90, 94–96, 99, 123–24, 125
Alexandria, Virginia, 60–61, 117, 123, 124–25, 126
Allen, Stephen, 103
American Anti-slavery Society, 146
American Colonization Society, 147
Anti-slavery Executive Committee, 71
Anti-slavery Friends, 74
Anti-slavery Office and Reading Room, 11

Anti-slavery Society. *See* Pennsylvania Anti-slavery Society
assassination, 23
auction, 70, 72, 80, 125, 148
Aunt Laura. *See* Haviland, Laura Smith
Austria, 59
Avoyelles Parish, Louisiana, 31–32

baby, 18–21, 141, 142–43
Bailey, Frederick Augustus Washington. *See* Douglass, Frederick
bakery, 1–4
Baltimore, Maryland, 56, 72, 85–87
Baltimore Sun, 85–86
barber, 52, 86, 126
barking. *See* Gilbert, Charles
Bartlett, Matt, 47–48
Bass, Samuel, 31, 34
Bayliss, John, 35, 36–38
Bayou Beouf, Louisiana, 30
Bay Shore, Virginia, 103
Beecher, Henry Ward, 68
Beloved (Morrison), 122
bidding. *See* auction
Big Dipper, 49
Bigelow, Jacob, 111–13, 114
Bill (slave), 108–9

ABOUT THE AUTHOR

 **Tricia Martineau Wagner**, a North Carolina author and presenter, is a well-versed and entertaining speaker who brings history to life. She is the author of *It Happened on the Oregon Trail*, *Black Cowboys of the Old West*, and *African American Women of the Old West*. Ms. Wagner enjoys speaking at conferences and conducting hands-on, living-history presentations for schools around the country on the topics pertaining to her books. She is an experienced elementary school teacher, reading specialist, and independent research historian.

Tricia and her husband, Mark, live on Lake Norman, North Carolina. They have two wonderful children, Kelsey Merreck and Mitchell Dale, and a Brittany spaniel named Tiger. To learn more about Tricia, visit her at www.authortalk.org.